Against Creativity

Against Creativity

Oli Mould

VERSO
London • New York

First published by Verso 2018
© Oli Mould 2018

1 3 5 7 9 10 8 6 4 2

Verso
UK: 6 Meard Street, London W1F 0EG
US: 20 Jay Street, Suite 1010, Brooklyn, NY 11201

versobooks.com

Verso is the imprint of New Left Books

ISBN-13: 978-1-78663-649-2
ISBN-13: 978-1-78663-648-5 (EXPORT)
ISBN-13: 978-1-78663-647-8 (US EBK)
ISBN-13: 978-1-78663-646-1 (UK EBK)

British Library Cataloguing in Publication Data
A catalogue record for this book is available from the British Library

Library of Congress Cataloging-in-Publication Data
Names: Mould, Oliver, author.
Title: Against creativity / Oli Mould.
Description: London ; Brooklyn, NY : Verso, 2018. | Includes bibliographical
references and index.
Identifiers: LCCN 2018018796| ISBN 9781786636492 | ISBN 9781786636461
(UK
ebk) | ISBN 9781786636485 (export) | ISBN 9781786636478 ((US ebk)
Subjects: LCSH: Creative ability – Philosophy. | Creative ability – Social
aspects. | Creative ability – Economic aspects. | Common good. |
Individualism. | Neoliberalism.
Classification: LCC B105.C74 M68 2018 | DDC 153.3/5 – dc23
LC record available at https://lccn.loc.gov/2018018796

Typeset in Fournier by MJ & N Gavan, Truro, Cornwall
Printed and bound by CPI Group (UK) Ltd, Croydon, CR0 4YY

Contents

Introduction
What Is Creativity?

On a cold February night in New York City in 2012, I exited a Midtown bar with a friend, having just taken in a typical Broadway mega-musical. Before we had the chance to get our bearings, an unkempt man dressed in an ill-fitting bomber jacket and a New York Yankees beanie confronted us. My initial reaction was, I'm ashamed to say, one repeated countless times in cities all over the world when tourists encounter the homeless: an attempt to dodge the situation as quickly as possible. However, before I could formulate an excuse, he broke into song. He had the most exquisite voice. It would not have sounded out of place in the show I had watched that night.

Having been perhaps a *bit* more inebriated than I would like to have been, I can't recall the exact words, but it started with the line 'Don't be bashful, don't be shy, / Don't be afraid of this homeless guy.'[1] The lyrics included a request for money. He was (or so he sang) only a few dollars short of the price of a Broadway musical course in which he was going to be top of the class. I forget the rest of the song, primarily because I was too busy laughing and fumbling in my pockets for change. Could my money help him turn his life around and enter the magical and creative world of Broadway? Would his name soon be inscribed in neon above the bustling Manhattan streets?

I walked away from the encounter elated. Here was a guy down on his luck, sleeping rough in the streets, but possessing a talent for song, comedy and salesmanship. He had taken the situation he found himself in and capitalized on it artistically. He was engaging in music, dance and comedy, aping the stereotypical New York City street performer so ubiquitous in countless rags-to-riches stories. A homeless person becomes a street performer, becomes a Broadway extra, becomes the star, becomes rich and famous – proof that anyone can make it. He was being very *creative*, wasn't he?

The more I thought about it, though, the answer I hit on was *no*. Talented? Absolutely. Creative? No. To my eternal regret, I didn't ask about his life, but his story can't have been unique: back in 2012, there were approximately 45,000 homeless people in New York City (a figure still rising today).[2] He was living in a global city that has developed under a regime of capitalism in which severe (and ever-increasing) social injustices are inbuilt; because of these injustices people often have to beg, perform or rob people for money just to survive. This man clearly had a gift, and he was using it in a way that many others with similar talent use it: he was selling it. This man, who found himself without a home at the hands of a rampant, unjust and gentrifying urban market, was doing what he thought he must do in order to survive. He was using the talents he had just to scrape by, so he could perform the following day, and every other day, over and over again.[3]

Today, the system that causes homelessness – and the other related injustices: precariousness, racism and the emboldening of fascism, massive inequality, global health epidemics and the rest – is the very same system that tells us we must be 'creative' to progress. This is because capitalism of the twenty-first century, turbocharged by neoliberalism, has *redefined* creativity to feed its own growth. Being creative in today's society has only one meaning: to carry on producing the status quo. The continual growth of capitalism has become the prevailing order of life.

It has not always been this way. Creativity has been, and still is, a force for change in the world. It is a collective energy that has the potential to tackle capitalism's injustices rather than augment them. Creativity *can* be used to produce more social justice in the world, but it must be rescued from its current incarceration as purely an engine for economic growth. This book will expose how creativity is wielded for profit. It will outline the ways in which people and institutions are being told to be creative in order to proliferate more of the same. But it will also highlight the people and processes that are *against* this kind of creativity, in that they forge entirely new ways of societal organisation. They are mobilizing it in a different way. They are enacting a creativity that experiments with new ways of living, ways that conjure entirely new experiences that simply would not exist under capitalism.

A History of Creativity

Creativity has always been a slippery and nebulous concept. But strip away the millennia of etymological layering, and you are left with a kernel of truth: it is the *power to create something from nothing*. And it is a 'power' rather than an 'ability'. Being creative is more than the 'ability' to create something from nothing in response to a particular need or lack. Nor is it simply an ability to produce a new product that the market has deemed necessary. Creativity is a *power* because it blends knowledge (from the institutional and mechanistic level to the pre-cognitive), agency, and importantly desire to create something that does not yet exist.[4] Far from being reactive, it is proactive; it drives society into new worlds of living.

So rather than 'What is creativity?' the more pertinent questions become 'Who or what has that power and desire?' and 'What is the *something* that is being created?' In ancient societies, this power was always a divine power, a God that made the Heavens and the Earth. From traditional Judeo-Christian views of the all-powerful Creator God and the story of Genesis, to Ptah the Egyptian demiurge who brought the world into being by simply thinking it, the act of pure creation has been beyond human agency. Mere mortals were imperfect sinful beings, subservient to an Almighty who had ultimate and unlimited powers to build something out of nothing.

But since the Enlightenment, Western civilization began to dominate, colonize and exploit the resources of our planet. Religions that preached the denial of the self and subservience to an external 'other' creative power were incompatible with a need for a better, richer way of life. So people began to look inward for sources of creativity. According to the doctrine of the dominant faith of the Western world, Christianity, we were made in the image of God, and so we too had the power to create. Hence to separate ourselves from the rest of God's creation, we imbued *ourselves* with the power to create.

During the Enlightenment, thinkers such as Hobbes, Locke and Rousseau saw that human imagination and creativity was the path to progress, not a blind genuflection to an all-powerful God. Science was the way forward, not faith. As Nietzsche proclaimed, God was dead, and we had killed Him.[5] As a result, it was craftspeople, philosophers and scientists who were considered 'creative': those who laboured for a lifetime to hone their intellect and their skills (and passed those skills down through the generations) were bringing into being new ideas and tools that allowed us to progress as a civilization.[6] Humanity, not God, was creating something from nothing.

What's more, 'artistic' creativity and a broader appreciation of culture were marbled through everyday life; they were part of the commons. Music, poetry and art were not considered to emanate from creative 'genius' or a higher cultural plane, but were simply part of collective social life. Shakespeare, in his day, would not have been thought a genius at all: he would have been seen as a craftsman, a wordsmith whose work was to be appreciated, enjoyed and 'consumed' collectively.[7]

Although creativity was increasingly thought of as an individualistic trait, there were alternative schools of thought. Groups such as the Diggers and the Levellers in England in the mid-seventeenth century vaunted the commons as more important to human progress than self-interest. The intricate co-operation among a group tackling the complexities of sharing and maintaining land was considered very creative. It was a collaborative and collective creativity that encouraged equality between people. Cultural production and artistic endeavour were integral factors in the process of maintaining a just society.

But it was a mode of societal organisation that, even at the time, was under increasing pressure from a dominant mode of thinking that focused on self-interest, the hoarding of private wealth and a reliance on interpersonal competition (rather than mutual aid) to provide equality.

As European powers began to plunder more of the world, they became richer and richer. Fuelled by a growing capitalist way of life that encouraged self-interest over co-operation (catalysed by the Enlightenment doctrines of competition as a key factor in societal progress that spawned such ideologies such as social Darwinism) the wealthy merchants wanted to privatize the enjoyment they got from the 'artistic' culture they had experienced collectively. The greed and selfishness around which Western societies were increasingly being organized bred a new desire to horde land (often from collectives like the Diggers) and, crucially, cultural products.

So the wealthy began to commission great works of art, and the more impressive these were, the more status they granted the commissioner. In combination with a phase of romanticized individualism, we saw the privatization of creativity. The artist producing the work became increasingly important, a development that, over time, wrenched artistic production out of the collective social arena, individualized the creative process and gave birth to the modern conception of the 'creative genius'.

The onset of the Industrial Revolution further entrenched the divide between those who were able to 'consume' art and those who were not. The wealthy (merchants, factory owners, etc.) had more time and resources to consume culture, while the workers spent more time on the factory floors. With the onset of the printing press, and later photographic and cinematic technology, cultural production itself became industrialized. Adorno and Horkheimer, in their now seminal text *The Culture Industry*, argued that capitalism had enabled this mass-production of culture. It had entrenched a divide between a popular culture that numbed the masses into passivity, and a high culture that heightened the senses.[8] This separation of cultural consumption into popular and high art characterized much of the twentieth century's articulation of creativity: artists produced art worthy of the name, the rest was industrialized forms of

mass objects that had far more to do with machine-like production that it did creative genius. Schönberg and Picasso
were creative; the Hollywood studios were not.[9]

So creativity, or more accurately the *power* to create
something from nothing, had gone from being a divine
power, to a socialized and collective endeavour, to an individual characteristic that could be traded. Being creative
now had *value*. It was a character trait that was much sought
after by employers, businesses and governments; it was an
exchange value to be exploited. And this is where the UK
government plays an important role in the contemporary
etymology of creativity.

In 1997, Tony Blair swept into power. Much of the
Labour government's early success lay in embracing the
concept of 'Cool Britannia', an exultation of the UK's pop
culture and artists. In a reversal of the divide that Adorno
and Horkheimer viewed as indicative of capitalism's culture
industry, Blair's 'New' Labour party celebrated popular
culture and the creativity at its core. By doing this, New
Labour caused two major structural shifts in the socio-
economics of culture and creativity. It related to the 'people'
on a national level (with its championing of popular culture),
and moved the economy from post-industrial services to
the proliferation of knowledge-based work (of all skill sets,
ranging from call centres to start-ups). The former of these
structural shifts got New Labour the votes, while the latter
allowed it to advance a rhetoric of creativity as having an
economic value and to forge a brand-new growth agenda
based on knowledge, entrepreneurship and innovation.

In 1998, it created the Department for Culture, Media and Sport (DCMS) and set about formulating a remit for the '*creative* industries' from the remnants of an unfavourable and out-of-date *cultural* industry policy.[10] Using templates forged in Silicon Valley and Hollywood, where the profitability of intellectual property had been perfected (not least by an army of legal service professionals and a flexible, autonomous business model), this new UK government set about adopting a cultural production policy that championed its competitiveness, global reach and viability for UK plc.

It was a phenomenal economic success. The creative industries began to be championed as the UK's flagship sector. In 2016, they were estimated to be worth £84.1 bn to the UK economy, and employed around 2 million people.[11] Not even the global financial crisis of 2008 curtailed their growth. As this success became celebrated, countries all over the world began to replicate the rhetoric and use the language of creativity in their economic and political narratives. So much so that today 'creativity' is applied to more and more aspects of our lives.

Now, everyone is encouraged to be creative – at work, in our personal lives, in our political activities, in the neighbourhoods in which we live, in schools, in our leisure time, in the choices we make in what we eat every night, in how we design our CVs. We are bombarded by messages that by being creative, we will live better, more efficient and more enjoyable lives.

From line managers, corporate CEOs, urban designers, teachers, politicians, mayors, advertisers and even our friends and family, the message is 'be creative' and all will work out for the better. They eulogize that we now live in 'creative times' and we are encouraged by 'thought leaders' to free ourselves from the shackles of bureaucracy, centralized power and social straightjackets, and 'unleash' the inner creative entrepreneur. In doing so, we will create innovative products and services that will empower us in work and social life.

Moreover, we are told that this version of creativity is no longer the privilege of an elite 'genius' few; it is something that everyone has. Creativity can be found in unskilled amateurs, on the street, on the shop floor or in the waiting room. We are all invited to take part in this new democratic and liberating form of creativity and in so doing, we will create new (often digital) products and processes that will transform social and economic life.

Contemporary society is formulated, operated and maintained with creativity as the core source of progress. This is having a huge impact on everything around us, from the places where we work to the ways we are managed. The traditional corporate hierarchy is now a defunct system that negates creative activity. Governments are too bureaucratic and stifle innovative policy thinking. Regulation is the enemy of flexible, agile and creative work. Social services, charities and other third sector institutions are failing not because their funding has been drastically cut, but because they are not creative enough. Hospitals, schools and universities that fail do so because they are insufficiently entrepreneurial and can't adapt to a rapidly changing marketplace and digital technologies. With the onset of this language, institutionalized into terms such as 'the creative industries', the 'creative economy', and the 'creative class', creativity became *the* critical paradigm of economic growth.

The spread of this economized and capitalism-friendly version of creativity has been turbocharged by the infusion of neoliberal ideologies. Formulated in the intellectual cauldron of the Chicago School of the 1940s and '50s, neoliberalism has become one of the most prevalent ideological forces of our time. Various readings of neoliberalism have seen it viewed as a mixture of free-market economic thought, the elevation of self-interest as the guiding force of progress, minimal state intervention and, increasingly, invasive forms of biopolitical control.[12]

At its core, though, neoliberalism is about the marketization of everything, the imprinting of economic rationalities into the deepest recesses of everyday life. The political theorist Wendy Brown has argued that neoliberalism 'configures human beings exhaustively as market actors'.[13] Every decision we take then becomes an act of weighing up the costs and benefits of choosing one option over another. If I hug my child now, will it help her become a more confident and employable adult? If I go for a run now, will it mean I'm able to be more productive later? Swipe left or right for love? If I spend more time counselling this student will it increase my student feedback scores?

Seen as a means of societal organisation, neoliberalism was openly adopted by key world leaders in the '70s and '80s, notably Margaret Thatcher in the UK and Ronald Reagan in the US. One of their key tropes was the importance of the 'enterprising self'. It wasn't up to the government or society to help you out: if you wanted to succeed in this world, you had to unleash the inner entrepreneur. It is easy to see then how neoliberalism and the creativity rhetoric go hand-in-glove. Being creative today means seeing the world around you as a resource to fuel your inner entrepreneur. Creativity is a distinctly neoliberal trait because it feeds the notion that the world and everything in it can be monetized. The language of creativity has been subsumed by capitalism.

Capitalism's Creativity

The dominant narrative of creativity is one of creating more of the same. Contemporary capitalism has commandeered creativity to ensure its own growth and maintain the centralisation and monetisation of what it generates. Marx prophetically argued that capitalism does not see its limits as limits at all, only as barriers to be overcome. Its relentless pursuit of resources to exploit, and wealth to generate for the elite, means that the only creativity capitalism has is in destroying alternatives and turning them into fertile and stable ground for further growth.[14]

The social theorists Luc Boltanski and Ève Chiapello, in their work *The New Spirit of Capitalism*, have argued that in the world after the protests in Paris in 1968 (and the counter-cultural revolution of the '60s more broadly), capitalism's growth has become predatory.[15] It preys on the people, ideas, things and movements that are in direct opposition to it. By mobilizing the creative industries of advertising, branding and public relations, contemporary capitalism actively seeks out those who are opposed to it, and offers fame and fortune. In essence, capitalism *stabilizes* those movements, people and ideas that are 'outside' it by naming them. It brings them into the 'mainstream' and the broader public consciousness. It does all this to prep them for commercialisation. Many countercultural movements, from hippy culture to punk to skateboarding, have fallen foul of capitalism's lure of monetary reward. In the twenty-first century, this process of co-option has become intensely rapid, and in some cases, extremely crass.

Take for example the furore over an advert for Pepsi that aired briefly in early 2017. The advert is focused on a laughably generic protest march, whose participants carry placards with slogans such as 'join the conversation' and 'love'. A fashion model is taking part in a photo-shoot nearby, and spies an identikit male counterpart (complete with a Pepsi can, of course) in the rally who seductively beckons her to join in. She throws off the shackles of her manicured beauty by discarding a blond wig and smudging her perfectly applied lipstick, and joins the throngs of the protest. She then grabs a Pepsi can of her own from an ice bucket and hands it to a policeman who is standing guard alongside the rally. He sips the refreshing soda, nods approvingly to the fashion model and to his fellow law enforcers. Everyone cheers and hugs each other and the screen fades to black. 'Live Bolder. Live Louder. Live for now'. Drink Pepsi.[16]

The advert rapidly received opprobrium on social and mainstream media platforms.[17] At a time of intense anger in the US, with marches against Donald Trump's presidency and institutional racism in the police, this advert was a blatant co-option of protest aesthetics to hawk a sugary soda drink. With a less than subtle riff on the famous image of Ieshia Evans being handcuffed by police officers in riot gear at Baton Rouge in 2016, Pepsi sanitized protest and redirected the powerful imagery of urban-based activism away from the social injustices they are trying to correct, to selling more drinks. Deaths in police custody, and the oppression of protesters by police who used kettling, pepper spraying and wrongful arrests were (and still are) raw in the public imagination, and when Pepsi aped the protest 'look' for gain, the rebuttal was rightfully swift, and their retraction welcome.

But the very presence of such a branding exercise is symptomatic of how capitalism mobilizes its agitators as vehicles for its proliferation. Drawing on an advertising and technology industry that scours the social world for images, movements and experiences yet to be commercialized, capitalism's 'creative' edge leaches any possibility that these *could* be utilized to create alternative social worlds. Any movement (be it a countercultural group, protest movement, meme or activist ideology) that is looking to

14

destabilize capitalism is viewed as a potential market to exploit.

Hence, capitalism's 'creative' power does not create, it appropriates. It offers stability to dissenting voices via financial incentives, recognition, or even the promise of a rest from the emotional and physical exhaustion of constant resistive practices. But in so doing, those anti-capitalisms cease their destabilizing practices: they become fertile grounds that can be harvested for more profit. Indeed, this is how capitalism's appropriative mechanisms have been so successful; it is the creativity rhetoric fuelled by the ideology of self-interest, market logics and competition that has been wielded as capitalism's most potent weapon. It has become the very means by which capitalism can boast: 'There is no alternative.'

Against Creativity

The following chapters highlight the ways capitalism co-opts creativity for its own growth. Through the prisms of work, people, politics, technology and the city we will focus our attention on how everyday life is being saturated by a creativity rhetoric that actively discourages us to work 'creatively'; and move towards a horizon of impossibility beyond the appropriative capitalism of the contemporary world. This book is in opposition to the way in which we are told to be creative; it is against creativity.

But in highlighting the injustices of this articulation of creativity, I wish to show how there can be an alternative, perhaps revolutionary creativity; one that is about creating new phenomena to which capitalism is unaware. It is increasingly difficult to see, but there is a powerful force in the margins of society and in the fissures of the commercialized world that are *destabilizing* the ground on which capitalism's future is being harvested.

Creativity *should* be about seeking out those activities, people, things and ephemera that resist co-option, appropriation and stabilization by capitalism. More than that, it should be about amplifying them. It is this version of creativity that this book looks to champion.

1

Work: Relentless Creativity

Later in 2012, after my trip to New York, I visited the MediaCityUK site in Salford, near Manchester in the north-west of England. I was interviewing management personnel at the newly opened BBC studios about their relocation from London.[1] After the interview, I was given a tour of the facilities, some of which were still being constructed and finished off.

I was shown the state-of-the-art television studios and radio suites, and went behind the scenes at the BBC Sports and CBeebies departments, which had yet to be fully opened. As I was led around the building, what struck me was the vast open plan offices, and the lack of private work-spaces. There were 'breakout areas' with large, circular and colourful seating, and an abundance of screens, some rolling the BBC News Channel, some blank. I couldn't be sure, as it was obscured, but I'm almost certain I also saw a foosball table.

It was very reminiscent of the style of workspace that has become synonymous with US-based tech companies, particularly Google. I put this to my chaperone; I asked whether or not this layout was a departure from the previous workspace in London, and what the rationale was for configuring it like this. The answer was one I did not expect. He said that creative industry workers are a lot like male peacocks during the mating season; if they're not constantly showing off, they're not going to get anywhere in this business. So by getting them to work in the same space, where they can see each other's work, they are more inclined to produce better, more creative results.

At the time, I laughed appropriately and carried on taking in the surroundings and everything else my chaperone had to tell me about the intoxicating surroundings of this highly *creative* place. But looking back, this passing analogy was far more appropriate than perhaps he thought. For me, it represents almost perfectly how 'creative work' is conceptualized in business and government parlance. First, it highlights the individualization of creative labour practices, despite the rhetoric that it champions collaborative working. Second, these open-plan spaces that supposedly encourage the collision of ideas and people actually negate the need for a physical 'office' or 'workspace' at all. Third, it shows that to succeed in the creative economy, you need to be flexible, adaptable and dynamic, and whether or not you're in the office, you always need to be 'at work'.

But these three themes have come to dominate creative work. How is creativity thought of and implemented in the worlds of business and policy? What it means to be creative 'at work' is to produce *only* more growth of contemporary forms of capitalist production. At the same time, 'other' forms of creative work and economies that produce radically alternative, or indeed anti-capitalist, means of socially organized labour are being marginalized, destroyed and/or reconfigured for profitable gain.

The result is an increase in the precariousness of work, the destruction of home life, and the slow erosion of socialized labour models, or what Marx called 'communal production'.

Work has always been creative, but centuries of capitalist appropriation have leached the use value of all forms of labour (be that domestic, social, emotional and so on) into concretized means of wealth generation. Artists, musicians, coders, writers, bloggers, sculptors, crafters, designers, architects, scientists and other members of the 'creative class' are currently 'being creative' only in so far as they are producing new ways for capitalism to appropriate the world. What I will explore, however, is the idea that with some radical new practices, they *could* be used to revolutionize it.

We Are All Creative, Right?

To shed light on creative work, how it came to be conceptualized and mobilized, and how it is destroying socialized forms of labour and creative production, we need only look at the work of one man. The bestselling book *The Rise of the Creative Class*, written by the urbanist Richard Florida, was published in 2002 and radically changed the notion of creativity in business and political realms. Florida's argument was simple: everyone is creative. The new economic order, he argued, is fuelled by this creativity, but only a few people are able to use it for economic gain. So for a place of business to succeed, it needs to attract those who are able to make money from that creativity: those he called 'the creative class'. These were the talented and innovative individuals who were going to change the world for the better, one pay cheque at a time. They were people who defied the stuffy, overly-bureaucratic nature of 'normal' work life and preferred flexible working hours and dressing down for the office; perhaps they even spent a day or two a week working in a coffee shop. They craved autonomy and a less stifling management structure, and didn't always require financial incentives.

Gone were the days of the 'organizational man' that characterized workplace culture from the post-war period. As William Whyte's famous text argued, to get ahead in corporate America people (of course, usually men) needed to engage in the old-fashion Protestant work ethic – be hard-working, diligent, thrifty and obedient to higher powers. But in addition, he argued that only through collaboration does work become worthwhile. People need to 'sublimate' themselves to the group, which goes on to produce bigger and better results – more than would be capable by working individually.[2] The creative class shunned all this. Collaboration was important, yes, but only as a means to further individual aims and career goals.

Making up about a third of the workforce (41 million people in the US; subsequent replica studies in other locations repeat a similar statistic), Florida's creative class are often highly educated (59.3 per cent of them have college degrees, according to his figures), and are able to use their talent to generate economic possibilities for their companies, institutions and/or locality.[3] They are non-conformists, introverts, maybe even a little dorky; but they are able to generate different ways of thinking, new products and services to bring to the market. People in creative class occupations, he argued, will earn nearly twice as much and are remarkably resilient to economic recessions: estimates are that in the US, while service sector job losses after the financial crash of 2008 clocked in at 6.2 million, creative class job losses 'barely registered'. This is because creative workers are flexible and can adapt their work to changing macroeconomic conditions.

The creative class can also be more egalitarian than the working, service or agricultural classes. According to Florida, the creative class is 52 per cent female. However it is 80 per cent white, more than the national US average of 74 per cent.[4] So while everyone is creative, only a select few benefit from this economically. This dichotomy dominates his thesis.

But as many scholars have pointed out since his work was published, Florida is simply recasting the Marxist class divisions that created the systemic inequalities and injustices of capitalism in the first place.[5]

Throughout his oeuvre, Florida argues for a particular type of creative work that is the apotheosis of economic growth and social progress. This is not limited to particular sectors, although he is at pains to prioritize creative industries as 'core', but is more about the kind of work people do, wherever they happen to be. Creative work is good because it encourages growth, and all other work is not because it is boring and ultimately unfulfilling. It allows and indeed champions mobility of labour, rather than being 'stuck' in monotony. The creative class that Florida lays out with a curiously narrow set of empirical data (for example, his Bohemia Index identifies diversity simply by the proportion of gay men) is always measured against the 'non-creative' working class and the service class (or the manufacturing and service sectors).[6] Naturally, it is the former that is shown to be the most important, diverse, resilient and dynamic sector of the economic labour force.

Also, throughout his discussion of the creative class, not only are their economic virtues championed, but their consumption and living standards are nearly always painted as an inspiration for the rest of society. In one of his more (in) famous anecdotes from his own life he states:

> The person who cuts my hair is a very creative stylist much in demand, and drives a new BMW. The woman who cleans my house is a gem: I trust her not only to clean but to rearrange and suggest ideas for redecorating; she takes on these things in an entrepreneurial manner. Her husband drives a Porsche.[7]

Hence, as we are all inherently creative, if we can exploit that creativity even in service jobs, we will enjoy elite consumption patterns (particularly, it seems, the enjoyment of German luxury cars). The 'creatification' of all jobs is thus the key factor in social mobility and economic growth. In other words, working-class people can enjoy the benefits of the middle class if they just 'creatify' their work. After all, we are all creative; we just need to 'unleash' that creativity on the world.

It is no surprise then that national, regional and local governments, business leaders, charity managers and even rock stars fell over themselves to extol the virtues of the 'creative class': they acknowledged that it was the 'life blood' of the knowledge economy. Florida's work had a robust veneer of statistical justification with endless graphs and tables. It used rags-to-riches stories that captured the imagination. It appealed to a cosmopolitan elite by confirming their social and class biases. Crucially, to this day, the book is used to justify continued inward investment and gentrification, as long as it *looks* creative. Florida has provided a magic recipe for economic success, in which creativity is the fundamental ingredient.

In the intervening two decades, a lot has happened in the US (and the world) that has seen this thesis unravel. The financial crash. The subsequent sharpening of income inequality (at urban, national and regional levels). Gentrification and the accompanying social cleansing of inner cities. Not to mention the rise of the populist anti-cosmopolitanism, racism and fascism all the way to the White House. In his most recent work in 2017, *The New Urban Crisis*, Florida admits that much of the aspirational success of the creative class, and its perceived bohemian utopia, has not come to fruition. He freely admits: 'I found myself confronting the dark side of the urban revival I had once championed and celebrated.'[8]

A dark side, though, has *always* been there. The very inequalities that existed in cities that the creative class thesis was supposed to address were the very *same* inequalities that the thesis exacerbated; it had just recast those same divisions along lines of whether or not we are creative. While stopping short of a full admission of complicity, he says that he was 'startled and disturbed' to find that the influx of creative class professionals into an area caused house prices to rise precipitously, which rendered it unaffordable to all but an elite few.[9]

He goes on to say that the rise of President Trump and other populist leaders such as Rob Ford, the right-wing mayor of Toronto from 2010–14, has set back progressive urban movements by decades. A rise that came about, in part, because of the glorification of a style of consumption unattainable to all but the very few. So despite Florida's recent backtracking and his insistence that the acute inequality of the creative class thesis in action is a residual factor rather than a structural quality, the creativity rhetoric he boldly proclaimed is the new normal of development across the world.

In one striking example, Florida was invited to participate in a video call to a remote part of the Democratic Republic of Congo (DRC), on a former plantation. To a group of workers who were trying to set up an arts centre on the old site, Florida set out his thesis of the creative class and how it can ignite a new mode of working. He was questioned about how his 'formula' could work in the DRC and without a hint of irony he said: 'In the DRC, [which] isn't the wealthiest place on the planet, in a place that has struggled, you can place a new model.' A new model, of course, predicated on his creative class theory.[10] So even the DRC, a country ravaged by centuries of imperialism, whose natural resources are mined (using child labour) for the raw materials to make consumer products for the West, can be creative if only it follows the right model.

According to Florida and those who subscribe to and implement his worldview, creative workers are an essential part of any business, charity, government, public institution, or even family. Scan any job description and 'creative' will be one of the key required attributes. A quick search through any jobs listings, will show (for example) an advert for a nurse that asks: 'Could you be the highly motivated, creative, and effective Registered Nurse we are looking for?'[11] Or you'll come across an advert for a research assistant on a project on mental health at a leading UK university looking for someone with the 'ability to engage creatively and productively with mental health service users'.[12] In many sectors, including those not formerly viewed as creative industries (in these cases, health or higher education, respectively), creativity has become a vital attribute. There are even construction companies that look for 'innovative' self-employed builders.[13] And the fast-food outlet Subway is always on the lookout for (severely underpaid) 'sandwich artists'.[14] Socialized care, research rigour, the ability to lay bricks and making a sandwich are *recast* as creative activities.

So, whether you are a nurse, a researcher, a builder, a sandwich-maker or, yes, a fully qualified member of the 'creative class', you are required to be innovative, entrepreneurial and creative at work. Rather than freeing us from the shackles of monotonous, non-creative labour, it has become clear that the rhetoric of 'creative work' is merely a ruse that allows 'work-like' practices to invade our leisure, social and *non*-economic lives. Creatifying jobs, it turns out, does not lift menial non-creative work into the utopia of creative non-work; it brings to bear on *all* work the dogmatic and unjust nature of capitalism's interpretation of creativity.

Florida was right about one thing – we are all creative, but not in the way he thinks. We are all creative because that is what all labour is now recast as.

Individualization

In the early years of creative industry policy formulation, much was made of collaborative working. 'Creative' firms shunned the linear and hierarchical form of governance, and sang the praises of a 'flattened' structure. (I develop this idea in more detail in the chapter on technology.) Computer game companies in particular were analysed intensively and shown to have extremely innovative and progressive organisational models. Instead of management meetings, committees and sub-(sub-)committees, they held daily 'agile' or 'scrum' meetings or 'huddles', in which all workers came together (usually at the beginning of the day) to brainstorm activities, iron out potential issues and bounce ideas off each other.

In 2001, seventeen US software development companies met in Snowbird, Utah, to form the 'Agile Alliance'. They wrote a manifesto that championed the advantages of this way of working across the creative industries.[15] This more informal mode of inter-corporation communication was seized upon by other sectors and replicated in private and public institutions alike.

The perceived benefits were that it brought together more diverse, often conflicting opinions and experiences and led to better problem-solving and ultimately more innovative and creative goods and services. The mantra of 'collaborative creativity' became almost assumed, and it is now a given in any creative industrial policy.[16] Yet the collaborative nature of creative work that the policy documents and business managers are so keen to encourage does little to engender any true sociality or communal work beyond a surface-level veneer of collective individualization. It promotes collective work but rewards individual endeavours. Indeed, some studies have found that this 'agile' form of firm organisation is regularly 'undermined by senior management' and remains ineffectual against traditional structural forms of firm decision-making.[17]

Look at some of the world's creative industry success stories. Apple's success is supposedly built upon the genius of Steve Jobs, not the army of Chinese workers in Foxconn, the children mining the raw materials in the DRC, or the innovation in glass-toughness technology by Gorilla Glass.[18] Facebook's rise to global domination of social media is portrayed as the result of the determination of one man, Mark Zuckerberg, but he has been accused of stealing the idea while at college.[19] And without tax-funded government grants worth up to $5 billion, Elon Musk's Tesla empire would not exist.[20] These examples (and many more besides) cut to the heart of an inherent contradiction to the narrative of creative work: it often extols collaborative, 'agile', collective and co-operative working practices, but only rewards insular, atomized, self-interested and individualized work.

And the physical office and workspaces have adapted to this. Like MediaCityUK in Salford, the boundaries of individualized work are eroding, replaced with an environment that attempts to catalyse collaboration and networking. But, as my chaperone so eloquently outlined, this actually serves to ramp up our individualism by forcing us to 'perform' this collaborative work, rather than actually engage in it. Walk around any 'creative city' neighbourhood, and you'll find these kinds of spaces throughout the streetscape. For example Shoreditch, the beating heart of London's capitalistic creativity, has spaces called 'The Ministry of Start Ups', 'Techspace', 'The Cube', 'The Brew' and many others (none of which are cheap). Having worked in a few myself, I know they are modelled on a creative aesthetic straight out of the Floridian playbook. Long tables, breakout spaces, a café, repurposed industrial paraphernalia adorning the walls, play areas, arcade machines; they are specifically designed to create an environment that appeals to the thirty-something creative class. Almost like a second home. It's an intoxicating vision of just how 'free' work can be.

And this individualization-masked-as-collectivism (fuelled by the neoliberal ideology of the importance of the enterprising self) explains the rise of 'co-working spaces' as the model working environment. They take the open plan office idea out of the firm and make it available to all (or at least those who can pay the rental costs). Today, cities are awash with adverts for 'creative co-working' spaces (usually repurposed old factory buildings). They appeal because they hide the increasing individualization (and related precariousness) of work under a veneer of collectivity, with a seasoning of hipster kitsch subculture.

These kinds of spaces and the work they espouse are seen as critical by many urban and business leaders because they allow for the collision of different people, ideas and experiences. These spaces are eroding the barriers between work, rest and play. Indeed, from the perspective of employers, they are vital in reducing barriers to connectivity and collaboration. Collapsing the boundaries (physical and psychological) between the office, the home, the street, the café, and even the bed becomes a means of further profit generation. The traditional notion of the office becomes almost redundant. Why have an office (and pay below minimum wage for a zero-hour contracted migrant cleaner) if employees can work from home? Why should an employer pay for an extra hour's work when the worker will answer those emails on the way home? In fact, why should they pay a direct salary with all those costly in-work benefits? Why don't they pay for the work on a contractual or outsourced basis? Indeed, why don't they just offer 'exposure' and 'reputational capital' instead of actual money?

Under the pressures of the creative work mantra, it is already incredibly difficult to distinguish between work, rest and play.[21] Indeed the notion of 'work' is being replaced by a more nebulous notion of creativity; our entire productive selves and the relationships we keep are now geared toward producing things, ideas, experiences and services that capitalism can exploit. As the architectural theorist Douglas Spencer has argued: 'The old question of whether one lives to work, or works to live, is rendered seemingly redundant in the merging of the one into the other. This is accomplished through the practice of skills, habits and techniques required of both work and non-work within an overall schema of productivity.'[22]

This 'overall schema' is capitalism's narrative of creativity, and its raw materials can be found anywhere in daily life. You have as much chance of coming up with a new idea while you're praying, playing with your child or dreaming as you do while you're 'at work'.

This individualization, and the accompanying invasion into everyday life, is the fundamental shift in how labour is conceptualized in contemporary capitalism. Florida's mantra has given an excuse to companies that strip away layers of securitization and in-work benefits, to do so for the sake of 'allowing more (individual) creativity to flourish' (rather than for the *actual* reason of maintaining profit margins for the shareholders at the expense of workers' pay and benefits). It champions flexibility, agility and dynamism over institutionalisation, social formations, hierarchy and structure. It essence, it increases the precariousness of workers.

Precariousness

Freelance workers live extremely precarious lives. One freelance comedian and writer I know will often have to work gigs at the other end of the country on a day's notice. They will perform to near empty rooms (which is one of the more degrading things that can happen as a comedian) because they want to keep the company that's paying them on side. Their office is a coffee shop in a sports centre, or at least it was until the sports centre brought in paid parking. They have even had to cut a holiday short so as to do work for local radio. One month they may be able to pay the mortgage and feed their children, while another may see the overdraft increase. They have done work only to not be paid because it 'wasn't funny enough'. Multibillion-dollar companies have told them that there aren't the funds to pay the going rate, but it'll be 'good for the CV'.

The life of a comic has rarely come with a full-time salary (unless you make it onto prime time TV). But this story is not unique to this profession at all. Indeed it is becoming more frequent in more and more sectors. Many freelancers across the economy – artists, photographers, graphic designers, plumbers, locum doctors, cleaners and so on – go through the daily routine of scouring for work, pitching, living on a highly variable income and battling corporate behemoths just to get paid (although obviously some occupations, such as comedy writers, will struggle more than others). They may love the job, but also it is often the only way they can get compensated for what they do, such is the pervasiveness of this unstructured, agile, flexible and footloose 'creative work'.

According to the narrative, though, such flexibility is an important and unique working characteristic of the creative class. As Florida notes,

> The flexible schedule is partly a response to the realities of our lives today – in households with two working parents, for instance, someone might have to bail out early to see the children home from school. But it is also tied to the very nature of creative work. A lot of creative work is project work, and projects tend to run in cycles, with periods of crunch time followed by slower periods. Creative work requires enormous concentration; it also requires periods of downtime, even during the day. Many people tell me they like to work hard through lunch hour, then take a long run or bicycle ride in the afternoon to recharge themselves for the remaining part of their workday, which might extend well into the evening, amounting to almost a 'second workday'. Also, creative thinking is hard to turn on and off at will. It is an odd sort of activity: one often finds oneself percolating an idea, or hammering away desperately in search of a solution to a problem, only to see the answer clicking into place at unusual times.[23]

The ability to flow between work, a bike ride, work and then play characterizes the creative worker. Companies, public institutions, charities and governments often reduce the stability of work expressly to 'promote' creativity. This has been taken to an extreme level with the creation of contractual and employment arrangements that glorify the precarious nature of creative and, increasingly, other forms of work.

There are people on zero-hour contracts, long-term employers having their work outsourced to freelancers and self-employed 'associates' via agencies, and the increasing casualization of labour via temporary, short-term staffing. In attempting to capture the benefits of this kind of creative work, employers are doing away with costly labour support structures and repackaging the new streamlined contractual arrangement as 'flexible'.

To show this, we need look no further than the university sector. As employees of public institutions, university staff enjoy security and generous in-work benefits.[24] However, the marketization of higher education means that universities' academic labour forces have become incredibly polarized; not to mention the army of outsourced cleaners, caterers and serving staff, and the students themselves working zero-hour contracts. On the one hand there are the tenured, (often senior) secured research staff; on the other, the casualized, short-term and over-worked teaching staff.

The increasingly casual labour market makes it necessary for staff to move from one post to the next, often in far-flung parts of the country (or indeed the world). The constant shuffling between contracts and institutions means reduced time to focus on research as more hours are spent filing applications, drawing up new lecture material and shouldering the increased share of teaching (itself swollen by ever-rising student numbers and administrative structures). The willingness of university hierarchies to invest in longer-term replacements has been weakened by commercialisation of the university sector (as well as political uncertainty), and so the long-term trend is to plug teaching gaps with short-term, minimum wage and even zero-hour contracted posts, creating a vicious circle of more and more precariousness among early career staff.

In the UK 54 per cent of academics are on 'atypical' working arrangements, including variable and zero-hour contracts and other insecure means of employment.[24] Job adverts have been posted (and after much uproar, hastily taken down) that offered short-term teaching for below minimum wage. This compounds the stress on early career academics to the extent that mental health problems are at epidemic levels: 55 per cent of academics in the UK suffer from mental health issues, double that in the general population.[26] Stories of depression, stress and anxiety are all too common on academic social media, with the blame laid squarely at the pincer movement of rapidly increasing workloads and decreased work security. In 2011, a postdoctoral researcher, Francis Dolan, killed himself; his close friends and family blamed the stresses and precariousness of academic culture for his death.[27]

Academics occupy the 'super creative core', according to

Florida's thesis. They are 'thought leaders' and producers of knowledge that fuel economic growth; as such, creativity is a key characteristic of their labour practices. However, the 'flexibility' that such creative work affords is enjoyed by only a handful of elite staff, and is a curse to the rest. Dazzled by the idea of academics as pseudo-celebrities, the majority press on with precarious (over)work in the hope that it will secure longer-term, perhaps permanent contracts.[28] These precarious academics have been given and/or take on disproportionately large workloads, put off having children, forgo joining unions, and work second, third or even forth jobs, siphoning non-economic emotional energies into working practices. In short, the spectre of creative flexible working that is *expected* and *assumed* actually reduces the ability to be flexible and redirects precious emotional energy away from leisure, rest and play toward economic goals.

This polarization of the workforce into tenured, secure research staff and a precarious, casualized teaching cadre is symptomatic of capitalism's development of labour structures. This creates a 'race to the bottom' where ultimate flexibility, agility and mobility are rewarded.[29] These characteristics are more often than not forged in privilege, with deep-rooted classed, racialized and gendered contexts. In other words, unless you have a strong support network, deep pockets, and are geographically and sectorally mobile, then these working conditions simply entrench precariousness rather than allow for flexibility.

The most vulnerable people in society, who have no

choice but to accept these precarious working arrangements, have to adjust to the whims of the employer, further increasing their socioeconomic instability. They are already struggling to work in an employment system that is institutionally racist, sexist and ableist, and with the imposition of 'flexible' working arrangements, these struggles are exacerbated. But within the utopia of the creativity rhetoric, in which everyone is creative, there is no struggle, only the potential to apply your 'creative' energies elsewhere.

Flexible creative labour then, unbounded by physical space, can bring work life, and all its stresses, into the sanctity of home life. It is not unusual for the middle class home to have an office, a room where work can be conducted. Scour the designs for new build private suburban homes for example, and they now include a small office space.[30] While this can promote efficiency and reduce the need for a commute, it also blurs the emotional boundaries between work and home. This is potentially damaging for work-life balance and hence mental health, and it erodes the possibility of the home as an important geographical, emotional and psychological space of non-capitalist sanctuary.

'Working from home' is a process in which the former colonizes and in effect destroys the latter; it is a process of *domicide*.[31] This process has traditionally been seen as the physical destruction of the home (via urban conflict and warfare). It also denotes the process of home 'unmaking' by political and social forces that can result in homelessness, domestic violence and/or large-scale demolition of social housing.[32] More recently, work in this area has viewed political and economic forces as means of opening up the home as a physical and emotional space to exploit. The UK government's 'bedroom tax' (in which tenants see their housing benefit reduced if they are found to have a 'spare' bedroom) for example has been a deliberate attempt to link welfare payments to the number of bedrooms people have in their council homes.[33]

And now we can add to the suite of domicidal processes the imposition of 'creative work'. Chores around the home are now done in the name of maintaining 'work mode'. Cleaning the office room, making lunch, sorting out home deliveries during the day; there is a suite of domestic labour practices (not to mention household expenditure) that props up creative work. More damagingly, the gendered nature of domestic life means that women in the household will bear the brunt of this work.[34]

For example, on 10 March 2017, a routine video-based interview for BBC World Service gained global notoriety because during the interview (of a white man) in his home office, his young children burst in through the door behind him only to be dragged out by a clearly flustered wife.[35] The video spawned comedic parodies almost instantly, but it signified a deeper social issue at the heart of this kind of creative industry work. It was a dramatic demonstration of how the domestic life that so undergirds the (often) masculinized and carefully stage-managed spectacle of twenty-four-hour news crashed into the very media it helps to create. It exposed the range of domestic labour practices (in this case, child rearing) that supports the creative work that goes on in the home, and how little this goes recognized. Creative work therefore is domicidal because it further leaches the productivity of domestic labour toward its own proliferation. The home becomes a precarious *place* because it becomes an extended *space* of creative capitalist production.

Creative work makes us all more precarious. It reduces the need for a physical office space, in-work benefits, and long-term contracts, and intrudes into our leisure time, home life and emotional energies. In this respect it has inherently neoliberal characteristics because it is actively destroying any form of collectivized, public and social work. Creative work is *anti*social.

Antisocial Creativity

In February 2013, Robert Francis QC, a barrister working for the UK government, released a highly anticipated report that summarized an inquiry into the multiple failings of a hospital run by Mid-Staffordshire Hospitals Trust; failings that led to many unnecessary deaths, abuse of patients, and horrific safety and sanitary conditions. The report highlighted how the hospital's management was wholly inadequate, had put corporate profits ahead of patient welfare, suppressed whistle-blowers and didn't do enough to address the declining levels of care.

The report called for large-scale organisation and cultural changes not only to this trust, but across the NHS in the UK. However, the report came at a time when drastic changes had already been made to the NHS, turning it from a wholly public and humanitarian health system that was 'free at the point of use, from the cradle to the grave' into a privatized, profit-making corporation by stealth. From the early 1990s, successive UK governments have introduced public finance initiatives (PFIs) within the NHS. These allow private companies to finance the construction of hospitals and then lease them back to the public sector, but in so doing saddle them with crippling levels of debt which they have to pay back (rather than reinvesting in further care provision).

Mid-Staffordshire became a Trust in 2005 and a PFI arrangement was signed to build a new entrance to the hospital. The £10 million debt accrued under this scheme led to the introduction of an additional management layer to the trust in an attempt to manage the financial intricacies of the hospitals, taking away resources that would otherwise go toward patient welfare. One hundred and sixty frontline jobs were cut in 2005 and 2006, and the accident and emergency department was closed at night.[36] Gaps were filled with agency staff who lacked proper training. The lacuna of trained nurses, carers and cleaners, and cuts to building maintenance, produced an unacceptably poor level of patient care, and ultimately to the patient abuses and unnecessary deaths.

While the Francis Report rightly called out this abuse and the shocking level of substandard care, it failed to go further and highlight that all this came about because of the drastic cost-cutting exercises in the face of huge levels of PFI-imposed debt. As a result, many trusts in the UK continued to adopt PFI schemes. Furthermore, the NHS is being encouraged (or forced by government policies) to codify performance with league tables for waiting lists, patient satisfaction feedback surveys and the intensification of laborious auditing practices throughout the organisation.

In addition, NHS workers are being directed by governance structures to operate like creative industry workers. They are told to innovate their services, use digital technologies, and come up with creative solutions to provide 'better' care for patients. But these directives are used as a rod to beat further 'efficiency savings' out of an already under-funded system. Writing for the *British Medical Journal*, the health secretary, Jeremy Hunt, said the NHS has 'inflexible employment models' and needed to be 'creative, ingenious and above all, flexible'.[37] He even suggested using employment apps modelled on those used in airline companies; as if hiring healthcare workers to tend to the patients whose chances of survival are greatly increased by intensive long-term care, is the same as finding someone to work on a long-haul flight.

This conflation of healthcare and more traditional service sector jobs is another characteristic of how the creativity rhetoric is seeping into the NHS. And all this comes at the expense of patient care because patients are treated like customers of the service industry; they are being *commoditized*. From the point of view of production, the forced shift toward the flexible *individualization* of work is destroying the socialized labour of medical and health care. And from the point of view of healthcare itself, patients are being treated (and hence behaving) more and more like customers.

In the *Grundrisse*, Marx identifies communal labour as that which does not pass though a mediated form of 'exchange value' (i.e. money) in order for its social value to be realized. More than simply producing 'free goods', however, communal labour is inherently social from the outset. Its exchange value is already realized before any production takes place – that is to say the NHS as a product is 'paid for' by its users via the taxation system universally before any need for healthcare is experienced. So the labourer partakes in a more socialized, less exchange-value producing form of work. Put bluntly, they don't work to make more profit for their employers. This is the 'publicness' of the NHS, and indeed is similar to state education, legal aid, the police and fire services and so on.

The history of nation-building in the NHS since the Second World War has a non-financialized social ethos embedded within it (or at least, it did). Nurses and doctors who signed up to work for it did so because of a commitment to improving the health of the population. Its *modus operandi* was one of public service. Believe it or not, many NHS workers still adhere to the mantra of a communal, public and social institution that is held together by a communal public and social labour value. Their belief is that healthcare cannot and should not be commoditized; patients are not customers.

However, decades of NHS reform have eroded the 'publicness' of the NHS, reducing its communal labour ethos and further commoditizing patient care. The introduction of codified targets, institutional auditing, and standardized care models have brought on a Fordist style of production and consumption. As the sociologist Richard Sennett has detailed:

> Fordism monitors the time doctors and nurses spend with each patient; a medical treatment system based on dealing with auto parts, it tends to treat cancerous livers or broken backs rather than patients in the round.[38]

This piecemeal approach to healthcare is a sign of the wider shift to individualization of production in the economy to increase profit. And it is a concern among many practitioners in the NHS. Many hospital doctors bemoan the recent impositions of micro-management techniques (targets, auditing, etc.), which have eroded the 'team ethos' that used to be very common on hospital wards. Weekend staff, for example, would often work regularly together, they would know each other's skills and, crucially, they knew their patients longer-term (chronic) health concerns.

Similarly, because of cuts to GP services and the outsourcing of auxiliary social care to private companies, community nurses linked to specific practices are very quickly becoming a thing of the past. They would go into people's homes, be privy to their longer-term needs, and become familiar with their personal and familial circumstances. Today, much of this is conducted by private agency social care workers often on zero-hour, minimum wage contracts. Healthcare is more than sorting out an acute specific problem. It involves hundreds of hours in social care, mental health provision and counselling, something which the atomisation of the NHS's provision is negating.[39]

Within public institutions, workers are not quick to change their culture to one of wealth-generation: communal labour is a check on the process of profiteering. But as corporate agendas have crept in via constantly-shifting management structures, a clash with this communal labour ethos has emerged. This has led to a polarization of rationales within the NHS: a governance structure that is looking to 'mediate' (to use Marx's terminology) communal labour with ever more flexible, service-style working practices and a system that commodifies the patient; and a workforce clinging on to a view of communal labour exchange. This duality of thought is being played out and exacerbated by an equally polarized media landscape that on the one hand eulogizes the sanctity of the NHS's publicness, and on the other sees this as blind faith that stops private capital and competition from saving the NHS from its ills.

The political struggle for the NHS is a critical factor in how the 'truly' creative labour practices in the institution develop. The staff are often heralded as the 'backbone' of the NHS. This includes the frontline surgeons, doctors, nurses, healthcare assistants, physiotherapists, cleaners and meal deliverers who maintain the day-to-day activities of NHS activities, and are the ones with whom patients and visitors will have most contact. In mainstream media portrayals of these people, there is of course the occasional narrative in which healthcare workers are rightly vilified as uncaring abusers, usually in the light of an undercover investigation. However, in the majority of media narratives, the NHS staff are heralded as dedicated, saint-like figures who are almost superhuman in their compassion, humanity and willingness to go above and beyond the call of duty.

NHS workers will often work well beyond their contracted hours (often at home), study and train in their spare time, spend their own capital on professional development, and be invested in 'the cause' of their work of providing healthcare to the general public.[40] These characteristics are the very same eulogized by Florida as defining creative class professionals, *but with one crucial and exceptional difference*: the value of their labour is 'communal' rather than defined by individualized desires and/or private profitable gains.

In other words, the 'value' of NHS workers' labour goes toward creating a collective, communal and, crucially, public healthcare service that is free at the point of use. They collectively perform the communal labour of universal healthcare, and give this over freely to the public. The Florida view of creativity sees this labour individualized and sold in accordance with market forces. But NHS workers are pushing against this and creating spaces for non-capitalistic healthcare provision to flourish.

At least some are, for now. And it is those nurses, doctors and other frontline staff who are utilizing their 'extra' (which, in a Florida-style language, could be recast as 'creative') capacity to intensify the communality of healthcare. Indeed, in the face of chronic underfunding, workers 'going the extra mile' is how the NHS manages to currently maintain its day-to-day service.

In 2016, the junior doctors of the NHS undertook a number of strikes in protest at the imposition of a new contract that would see them working more antisocial hours on irregular shift patterns, imperilling patient care. Despite a number of media attempts to smear the doctors as greedy and simply after a pay rise, public support for them remained stubbornly high, and they had support from across other medical professions.[41] So when media narratives portray NHS workers as 'superhuman', it is the fact that these workers are utilising their extra personal and social resources towards a non-commercialized, non-capitalist public service which is so extraordinary, precisely because it is increasingly rare in contemporary capitalist society.

In very different circumstances, a similar story emerged in the aftermath of the Grenfell Tower fire. The firefighters, police and paramedics were all rightly praised for their unwavering commitment to tackling the fire and tending to the wounded. Pictures of exhausted firefighters, having worked up to twenty-four hours straight, flashed across social media, and they were lauded as heroes of public service, giving their all for the continued provision of public safety in the face of immanent fatal danger. It seems that to be superhuman in today's world is to work for a cause that doesn't contribute to capitalism's growth.

Within the NHS, the 'products' of waged labour, that's to say the care received by patients, are not socially quantifiable and they are certainly not measured against each other.

Making someone healthy again has no intrinsic monetary value. Of course, neoliberalism would say otherwise and attach a productivity figure to being well again; as if returning to health is worth it only if you can go back to work. Much like education, fire services and other public services, healthcare in and of itself is inherently socialized and communal in its production and consumption. We all have or will require healthcare at some point in our lives, and so the workers of the NHS are constituents of a *communal world* that healthcare provides, a world that does not see competitive market forces determine who gets healthcare or not. In this world, patients are given more holistic, continual and humanized forms of care. Work that goes towards the *continual* production of this communal world is what is truly creative.

True Creative Work

Creativity could be – indeed, should be – thought of more as an emancipatory force of societal change. The NHS, despite being encircled by the wagons of private capital, still maintains a socialized and communal work ethos. Rather than adhere to individualized forms of work and codified consumption, the NHS and other public institutions can encourage more socialized and communal models of labour. This will produce new patterns of social work that are less precarious and more equitable.

For real creative work to be championed, we can look to models of co-operative working arrangements that utilize communal labour and assets free from the spectre of privatization.

For example the *recuperadas* movement in Argentina after the 2001 financial crisis serves as a good illustration of how a large-scale movement of exploited labourers can 'reclaim' a bankrupt and foreclosed factory, fire the bosses, and reorganize the institution from the bottom up. Far from turning to a trade union to fight their battle for them, they organized themselves without hierarchy or direction from 'above'. All the workers were paid the same wage, and management decisions were taken democratically. It was not an occupation of factories to demand that they be reopened: it was far more radical than that – it was the occupation and *recuperation* of its productive processes.[42] This echoed many attempts at workers' action groups that militantly recaptured the means of production from the factory owners.[43]

In this sense, a politics of collective action involves conscious and combined efforts to build a new economic reality, one that is more equitable, less exploitative and more communal. Co-operatives such as those in Argentina can be found all over the world, and we see them in neighbourhoods, communes and even in the commercial sector. For example, there is Coffee Cranks Cooperative in Manchester UK that both owns and controls the workspace, with their website stating they are 'establishing an economic alternative to the biased economic system we find ourselves in'.[44] There is a thrift shop in Glasgow and a bike repair shop in Oxford among many other businesses in which all workers have ownership of the store, pay is more equitable, and the workers are engaged in community-focused activities.[45]

The Mondragon University in Spain is a much larger co-operative in which the management structure is made up of a group of thirty students and early career staff. Like the factories in Argentina and the retail outlets across the UK, they have a 'flattened' pay structure. No staff in the university earn more than three times the lowest wage, and each member of staff buys into the university after working for two years, an investment that can be taken out upon retirement. In addition, all staff can see each other's expenses, and departments will help to bail each other out financially if they struggle to attract funding.[46] It is a private university, so students do have to pay fees up front, but from the point of view of institutional labour models, it is very much against the grain of contemporary public institutions elsewhere, particular in the UK. Equitable pay structures, transparency in expenses and fair retirement packages are a far cry from the recent controversies surrounding the pay of the UK's university vice-chancellors and indeed other high-level management positions of public institutions, the media frenzy around the exposé of MPs' expenses, and the pension scandals engulfing some corporations.

But the history of co-operative working arrangements is haunted by capitalism's attempts to extract surplus value and appropriate these more equitable working arrangements into profit-making machines. Henri Lefebvre described how this is resisted with the process of 'autogestion'; when a group of workers try to 'master its own conditions of existence', free from externalized control.[47] The process of autogestion has been used to describe the *recuperadas* in Argentina, as well as Occupy, squats, communes and other marginal societal organizations.

Autogestion includes elements of centralized control and bureaucracy, which the workers must then absorb and redistribute. It is not a utopian model of perfectly equitable working practices, but is it an 'opening towards the possible' that allows workers to take control of their production and their own lives free from the perceived inevitability of corporate capitalist labour models.[48]

One of the most important refrains in Marx's work (and many of the philosophers who built upon his work) is that the human desire to work and produce is innate; it dwells within us all. It is a fundamental desire to create new worlds, experiences and subjects. As the feminist geographer Gibson-Graham has argued, 'work' produces more than exchange value and money: work can produce emotional support, protection, companionship, and a sense of self-worth.[49] Those factory workers in Argentina needed to work, not only to feed and clothe their families, but to maintain a sense of purpose, of being-in-the-world. Mondragon University's staff could well be paid more in other universities but invest in the co-operative equity of the institution. And NHS staff work well beyond their contracted hours because of their dedication to the improvement of public health and well-being. In any articulation other than that of contemporary capitalism, these are 'creative acts'.

But, as has been shown thus far, the capitalistic processes

that prey on those types of creative acts have shifted the ethos of 'creativity' to one that entails the production of the same capitalistic processes. In other words, creativity under capitalism is not creative at all because it only produces *more of the same* form of society; it merely replicates exiting capitalist registers into ever-deeper recesses of socioeconomic life.

And it is this version of creativity that must be resisted. By organising co-operatively and engaging in autogestion, communal labour can be engaged in without any extraction of labour value for the sake of profit-making. Communal labour and co-operative working arrangements that are radically equitable *destabilize* the waged labour process by providing more heterogeneous forms of working practices. Co-operative models of labour organisation, self-management and equality of pay; these are the antitheses of the current vernacular of creative work, but they should be its driving force.

But capitalism always strives to appropriate these autogestive behaviours. It shifts the *idea* of collaboration away from a shared ethos of communal and equitable production, toward a mere collection of already commoditized labourers looking to get out more of what they put in (like those seen in the 'Agile Alliance'). In addition, the creativity narrative itself has offered 'remedies' to the growing injustices of creative work. Florida has gestured toward the noble sentiment of a 'Creative Compact', one that is 'dedicated to the *creatification* of everyone.'[50]

He acknowledges the problems of polarization and the

immiseration of the service class, but his panacea is for every worker 'to harness his or her own inner entrepreneur'.[51] This can be done, it seems, by simply paying more for the products of the service class: 'if we paid more for cars and consumer goods, why can't we pay a little bit more collectively to the people who prepare our food, look after our homes, and take care of our children and aging parents?'[52]

Florida goes on to suggest that in this Creative Compact, there is a need to adapt the existing models of incubator spaces, business accelerators and other forms of co-working spaces, to service class professions. There is also a need for a social safety net for the creative economy, one in which healthcare, pensions and work benefits move with the worker, rather than with the employer. The education system also needs to be revamped to prioritize creative activities.

It would seem then to Florida that any problems could be solved by more consumption. However, maintaining the model of consumption, exchange and labour exploitation via wages will not bring about this 'creatification': quite the opposite. As Marx explained:

> It is clear, therefore, that the worker cannot become rich in this exchange [wage labour exchange between a worker and employer], since, in exchange for his labour capacity as a fixed, available magnitude, he surrenders its creative power.[53]

The creative power Marx alludes to could bring about alternative social formations beyond the formal exchanges under capitalism. However, 'creative work' in its current usage does not, indeed cannot, realize this. It is locked into the exploitative systems of waged labour. We can pay as much as we like for our services, but unless there is a radical shift in the way the use value of these services is realized (for example, via communal labour and co-operatives), then the conditions that create the polarization, exploitation and precariousness will continue.

Creative work, under capitalism, is only valid if it is used to facilitate capital's expansion and to shut down viable alternatives. For creative work to be utilized in the (re)production of an economy that is equitable, it needs to be wholly redefined. It has become a trope within discussions of creativity that 'everyone is creative', just that some of us are lucky enough to be rewarded financially for that creativity. But if this creativity is to be rewarded *ubiquitously*, then it needs to be used in the service of building social formations that do not rely on the exploitative nature of capitalist exchange.

The geographer David Harvey, channelling Marx, has consistently argued that capitalism's growth mechanisms are predicated upon the creation of a linear progressive view, one that blinds us from realizing other modes of social formation. He argues that 'we foreclose on revolutionary possibilities if we blindly follow that norm and replicate commodity fetishism. Our task is to question it.'[54] Creative work, despite its evangelists, does little to question the norm of capitalist accumulation: indeed it catalyses it. To break from this norm, and realize alternative modes of organizing societies and economies, is what creative work can allow us to do – it just needs to be 'released' from the vernaculars in which it is currently embedded. Rather than 'releasing the inner entrepreneur', creative work can, and should, 'release the inner revolutionary'.

2
People: Marginal Creativity

Sometimes, the most 'creative' acts stem from the collision of two or more seemingly disparate ideas. In 1903 Lizzie Magie, an American board game designer (and part-time political activist), filed for a patent for her latest creation, The Landlord's Game. Players took it in turns to move around a circular path (most board games were linear at the time) and conducted acts of 'labour' on each turn. After passing the Mother Earth square, they received wages. However, if players landed on a square owned by another player, they were charged rent. Money could be borrowed from a central bank, and indeed other players, but when it ran out, players went to jail or declared bankruptcy. The game went on until only one player was left with a monopoly over the board.

Magie also taught political economy, and was an advocate of the economic philosophies of Henry George. This included a belief in a single tax system for owners of property. She believed that the world around her at the turn of the twentieth century had become more unequal because of rapacious mercantilism, and wanted to spread the Georgist message that a more equitable form of taxation would be a remedy to societal ills. So using her creative talents as a game designer, she brought the mechanisms of this taxation system to bear on the leisure pursuits of middle class homes and created The Landlord's Game. At first the game was passed around friends and neighbours. It proved popular among a certain (politically progressive) demographic, but never crossed into the mainstream.

That is until 1932, when the story takes a more familiar turn. Charles Darrow was playing it one night and was so engrossed (and desperate for money) that he tweaked the game slightly and decided to sell it. Parker Brothers bought the rights under a new name, Monopoly.

Magie was initially thrilled to see a version of her game in production, but having been given only $500 and no royalties for her part in its creation, she become increasingly disappointed. She spent the rest of her days as a receptionist, earning little more than the living wage. Monopoly remains one of the most popular and most profitable board games today, and Darrow died a multimillionaire.[1] Darrow, and the corporate ethos he engendered, had taken a progressive, quasi-critical product and turned it into one of the most recognisable brands in the world that encourages a mind set of total competition, a winner-takes-all mentality.

But this story also highlights two specific and nuanced traits in this process. The first is the way in which creativity can come about via the collision of two different 'realms', and how this collision can create new ideas, products and experiences. The second is more insidious. Magie's identity as a woman (unmarried at that) in a highly masculine and conservative society meant she was actively marginalized from the rightful rewards that her creativity should have afforded.

How do these two processes play out in contemporary narratives of creativity? As the previous chapter detailed, individualization is a key factor in the contemporary rhetoric of creativity. But the rhetoric demands even more; you have to be a particular *kind* of individual. Too often it is white, middle-class, straight, fully abled men that are creative and innovative, and all other forms of minority identity are further marginalized. And in the case of Magie, their ideas are stolen and/or co-opted for profitable gain by profit-seeking men. Yet, these 'minor' subjects are *truly* creative in that they are experiencing the world in ways 'beyond' the majority: they can forge new ways of being that are, as yet, *un*appropriated, and show us different worlds that are within reach.

Creative Collision

In 1964, Arthur Koestler published *The Act of Creation*. In it, he outlines how the creative process consists of 'bisociation', the act of colliding two or more matrices, or 'planes', he says, in order 'to make a distinction between the routine skills of thinking on a single "plane", as it were, and the creative act, which ... always operates on more than one plane.'[2]

These planes (which he also calls 'frames of reference') are previously incompatible but collide when an act of bisociation brings the boundaries crashing down and allows their inner workings to change. For Koestler there are 'codes of disciplined reasoning' that inhibit the chance of bisociation, and hence stifle creativity. Very human traits such as habit and common sense, but also broader 'dogmatic' narratives of social norms, can act as frames that constrict particular ways of thinking. It is only when an idea, an act, a play on words or a piece of art (or perhaps a board game) brings together two or more of these planes that these codes are subverted. For example:

> The laws of disciplined thinking demand that we should stick to a given frame of reference and not shift from one universe of discourse to another. When I am arguing about Richard III and somebody quotes 'my kingdom for a horse' I am not supposed to shift my attention to my chances of drawing a winner in the Grand National, however tempting it may be.[3]

Take the simple pun, says Koestler. Punning is an act of creation because its purpose is to bisociate two frames: in this case, for the purposes of a joke. Koestler explores science, art and humour to show how history is littered with acts of creation that have blazed the trail of human knowledge.

However, in reading Koestler's work and the creativity narratives that stem from it, a question arises, which is: why (or where) are these 'frames of reference' separate in the first instance?[4]

There is little doubt that many of the world's most 'creative' moments in science, art, politics and indeed board games have come from bisociative action, but there is a broader philosophical question as to how those modes of thought came about. Let's take the example he offers of the phrase 'my kingdom for a horse'. Uttering these words can indeed make (some of) us immediately think of Shakespeare, with all the weighty and dramatic ideas his work conjures; but only if we have been exposed to his works in the first place. In other words, there is a *process* of socialisation that includes educational attainment, cultural development and indeed a working knowledge of the English language that links 'a horse, a horse, my kingdom for a horse' with a 'particular frame of reference'. But the process is always in flux. If the educational syllabus changes, Richard III is consigned to oblivion. Cultural touchstones shift. Language evolves.

Those frames of reference which Koestler assumes to be rigid are far more fluid, porous and flexible than we imagine. Furthermore, the act of framing the references in the first place is a political process. The presence (or not) of Shakespeare within national syllabuses is a governmental (and hence always debated) decision, and his presence in syllabuses in other countries is a process largely associated with colonial practices of the British Empire. Also, the evolution of language is contested often along class-based lines. Slang, text-speak, abbreviations, and changes in spelling are often vilified as an affront to a language – an insult to the Queen's English. Yet, this often masks class-based attacks: those who use these 'new' languages often are working class, the urban poor or simply the younger generation. So for Koestler, a pun collides two frames of linguistic reference (Shakespeare and horse-racing), and exposes the often politically charged coming-into-being of these references in the first instance.

The creative process that Koestler outlines so vividly is creative not because it fundamentally changes broad, immobile and complex social realms. Rather, it is creative because it *destabilizes* the processes that maintain the *perceived* rigidity of those planes in the first place. It is a creativity that critiques the 'normal' functioning of these processes and offers new ways of thinking that subvert these processes to create alternative ways of viewing the world. The realms that are so stable in Koestler's theory are only identifiable as such because of continual, political power that benefits from *stabilizing* them.

The stabilization of conflicting, politically charged and contested processes into a coherent and unproblematic norm characterizes contemporary articulations of creativity. Furthermore, the process of stabilization is made all the more palpable by the relentless focus on the individual as the key agent of change. Part of the neoliberal ideology is the 'individualization' of society, because it allows for the emancipation of the enterprising self. However, advocates of neoliberalism deliberately downplay the constant ebbing and flowing of social processes that go toward making up the individual in the first place. In other words, under neoliberal versions of creativity if you want to make a 'creative' change in your/my/a/the world, the power to do so comes from within, rather than through connecting with others.

While pretending to be looking for moments of connection, neoliberal versions of creativity champion individuality, and shun attempts to change the contexts in which individuals operate. Indeed, these contexts have become so granular that it becomes ever more difficult to relate, connect and mobilize into a collective force that could subvert and challenge them. The trick of neoliberal creativity then is to convince us that you can only be creative by looking to your own agency; any appeal to wider structures do not matter. Any semblance of the social has collapsed into and onto the individual. Life has been broken up into smaller and smaller constituent parts whose relations become more opaque, codified and/or hidden.

This version of creativity therefore is fuelled by the intense atomization of the everyday. In effect, individual agency is all that we can rely on because the social world is crumbling before our eyes. Creative people are hyper-individualistic. As the previous chapter outlined, collaboration is important for sure, but not at the expense of foregoing self-interest as the main purpose for that collaboration. Working together is only worth it if it benefits those involved more than if they were to perform on their own. There is no lasting collective solidarity.

Returning to Florida's work, we can see that this is one of the fundamental problems with his collectivization of the creative class. The very word 'class' implies the exact opposite of their much-vaunted *raison d'être*. They work to individualize and atomize the socioeconomic world, rather than to make fellow cause with other exploited workers so as to redress the sources of that exploitation. The individual is the sole agent of creativity.

This narrative is taken a rung higher by the management and business guru Adam Grant with his 2016 book *Originals*. It charts the stories of people who follow the economic path less travelled and 'take the initiative to make their visions a reality'.[5] The book opens with a vignette of Grant's refusal to invest in Warby Parker (the now billion-dollar online retail company) when it was a start-up, and argues that a group of people, 'the originals', are the true innovators of the world. They procrastinate a bit, aren't always the first ones to implement the idea, and actually have a back catalogue of distinctly average ideas. As Grant has said:

> It's much easier to improve on somebody else's idea than it is to create something from scratch. To be original, you don't have to be first. You just have to be different and better.[6]

These originals are not always the maverick, risk-taking leaders that have come to stereotype the idea of the world-changing innovator. People such as Steve Jobs, Mark Zuckerberg, Larry Page, Sergey Brin, David Gilboa, Neil

Blumenthal or, indeed, Charles Darrow have founded their financial success on a 'gradual', progressive and perhaps less explosively innovative event, rather than an Archimedes-style Eureka-moment.[7] Grant's work extols the virtues of questioning default ideas, of engaging with different audiences and constantly looking for ways to change the status quo. But he is clear to point out that these originals are not 'different' to the rest of us; they are not genetically disposed to be more entrepreneurial. They have the same fears and doubts that we all have, and if we follow a blueprint of their thinking, we too may be able to be an 'original'.

Grant's ideas, and many more like them, have come to typify a body of management literature that explores the best ways to replicate the success of billionaire entrepreneurs. These self-help business manuals are often suspicious of herd-like behaviour, and argue that following the crowd and the damaging tendency to 'group think' only ossifies the prevailing order and diminishes your ability to be 'an original'.

Moreover, for Grant and the narrative that he champions, context doesn't matter. Whatever the field you're operating in, having the right mix of characteristics will allow you to be 'original'. Art, science, civil rights movements, national government, community empowerment, queer politics, feminism: they are all stripped of ethical, political and moral content and reduced to homogeneous realms that can all be innovated *in the same way* in order to 'drive change in the world'.[8] The socioeconomic, political and cultural contexts in which these vastly different, conflicting 'realms' operate are reduced to arenas with the same rules of engagement, arenas in which the self can operate, tinker and, if original enough, change entirely.

But if we refer back to the example of Lizzie Magie, she was acting as a true innovator, someone who was colliding highly malleable frames of reference in order to produce a creative artefact designed to effect a progressive change in the world. Yet her idea was essentially stolen (by a man) and appropriated by a corporation. The context of her identity as a (then) unmarried woman and the highly masculine and family-orientated social world she was operating in led to her exploitation. Rather than Magie being the central focus of the history of Monopoly, Darrow is, and it is he who will be remembered as the 'original' thinker in this story.

So context *does* matter. It matters because the entire concept of being 'original' was devised within exclusionary capitalist identity politics. To be original then requires a social privilege that is wrenched from these broader contexts. In the same vein as the creative class, those lauded for being original in the modern economy are those who have benefited from a social milieu in which their identity is privileged above all else. These people so eulogized as 'originals' are often educated in elite institutions, come from middle-class families in wealthy parts of the Western world, and will ordinarily have use of all their senses and limbs. They are unlikely to be the subject of institutional racism, ableism or sexism by educational institutions, the police, the courts or city management. They would almost certainly ape the characteristics of the state power brokers they lobby vociferously, and be able to fit in comfortably at a top level networking event. In short, they embody the identity of neoliberal capitalism. So, anyone can be the next Mark Zuckerberg, as long as you're male, white, middle-class and live in the West.

You also need to be fully able-bodied. Within capitalist society, the efficient working of the human body has been paramount to its progression. It is only when workers are 'fully' functioning, healthy and of sound mind that they are able to create as much surplus value from their labour as possible. So when the human body breaks down, when its daily functions are not aligned with the 'perfect' vision of corporeality (that is, white, male, adult, middle-class and fully abled) it is marginalized, oppressed and/or co-opted.

Critical scholars of gender and race have written accounts of the centuries of capitalist oppression of non-male and non-white bodies, and how these identities have been used to critique systems of oppressive white male power and form broader social justice campaigns.[9] But it is only relatively recently that disabled bodies have been thought of in a similar way (due to advances in medical science that allow for detection of physical, sensorial and mental disabilities).

Given how the capitalist discourses of creativity champion the 'perfect body' as the crucible of creative energy, where does that leave bodies that do not conform? Can these bodies be 'creative' without being normalized? Are they in fact *dis*abled at all? Or are there just different ways of being in the world? Are they *diff*abled? Perhaps it is disabled (or diffabled) bodies that are the true destabilizers; perhaps it is they who are truly creative.

Diffability

If you're reading this there is a very good chance you have the 'full' use of your eyes.[10] You will probably be able to see out of the nearest window and navigate your way around a city with relative ease by reading signs, making sure you don't crash into obstacles and generally being able to negotiate crowded environments. For those who are partially sighted, though, urban environments can be extremely hazardous, frustrating and sometimes even deadly. The design of the built environment is often extremely marginalizing for people with partial or full blindness.

But many blind people have learned to adapt. They use smell, sounds and touch to navigate the city. In so doing, the scent of a flower bed outside a house can be just as an important marker of location as the sight of that house is to a seeing person. They are more 'in-tune' with the built environment. The blind architect Chris Downey (who was born seeing, but went blind in his adult life) has said that his unsighted experience of the city is far more sensory than his sighted experience ever was. The feel of sunlight on one side of his face, the smells of different shops, the changing audio landscapes of the city are all far more vivid then when he was sighted.[11]

Indeed he goes on to argue that the city *needs* blind people. It encourages people to look out for one another, and if a city is designed with blind people in mind, the urban streetscape becomes more walkable and accessible. All this would not be known to Downey had he not gone blind. His blindness created new ways of experiencing the city from a personal sensory perspective, but also from a planning and design perspective. Diffabled people, then, have the potential to be radically 'creative' because they are attuned to and realize, and even to some extent bring into being, entirely new and alternative subjectivities that are beyond the normalized world.

There are two modes of thought within disability studies – the biological model and the social model.[12] The former considers disability to be a deficiency in the normal workings of the human body that requires a medical intervention in order to 'correct'.

This has been the over-riding medical view of disability for centuries. Entire industries have built up to create drugs, medical technologies and artificial body parts, all designed to give the recipient an ability that they lack in comparison to the 'normal' body.[13] The medical model sees disability as entirely internalized in the body, and in need of biological, chemical or technological interventions. Hence, people with depression are prescribed antidepressants and/or forms of therapy, those who cannot walk unaided are given wheelchairs or walking aids, those who are deaf are fitted with hearing aids or cochlear implants.

The social model of disability inverts the biological model to argue that a person's disability comes about from society's inability to accommodate their way of being. So, for example, the design of some city streets are disabling for blind users. The Hollywood film industry only makes films that overwhelmingly cater for fully-sighted, hearing people. Some schools don't get enough funding to equip themselves to teach children with autism. Rather than viewing disability as a deficiency of the individual, the social model of disability sees it as a product of society's condition to cater for only a particular kind of body and mental functioning: one that can walk unaided, has use of all limbs and senses and has 'normalized' mental capacities – essentially the kind of body that can engage in 'creative work'.

Let's consider deafness as a means of enabling people to experience the world around them in radically different and creative ways. Deafness is a condition that someone can be born with, or develop. There is a spectrum to deafness too, and those who experience severe to profound hearing loss can make use of technology to improve their hearing by the use of hearing aids or, at a higher level of complexity, cochlear implants. Both devices are attempts to allow deaf people to hear 'normally'. In the UK there are systems of health checks, new-born baby hearing screenings and national guidelines geared toward 'catching' deafness earlier on in life and allowing the child and the parents to be given options of medical interventions that would allow the child to hear; such interventions could be seen as part of the biological model of deafness.[14]

However, when viewed via the social model of disability, deafness becomes a product of a world with an innate aural bias, which manifests in social communications and spatial constructions. Deaf people encounter 'everyday' discrimination, particularly in service encounters with hearing people. So when deaf people cannot communicate according to social norms, they are often viewed as an annoyance, an obstacle or even as unintelligent. Indeed, such discrimination stems from a phonocentricism inherent within society: deaf people cannot hear, therefore they cannot experience everything modern life has to offer. This is a suppressive force on deaf people, preventing them from expressing their experiences of society.

By conforming to the hearing world's rules of engagement, those who cannot hear are forced to act disabled. The social model contends that disability is actually nothing of the sort – there is no 'dis', only difference. There is no disability, only *diffability*. It is this difference that allows for a radical view of creativity. But it is also a difference that is actively stunted by contemporary society.

Furthermore, within academic discourse, particularly the strand of 'deaf studies', there has been a debate raging about the difference between deafness (with a small d) and Deafness (with a capital D).[15] The former is considered to be the medical condition of not being able to hear as well as others. More importantly, it denotes a 'kind' of deafness that does not identify with a Deaf culture more broadly. Being Deaf (with a capital D) implies an immersion in the socio-cultural affiliations of the Deaf culture. The use of sign language, participation in Deaf social clubs, and attending Deaf schools are just some of the activities that help to formulate the Deaf culture. Many Deaf people will argue that the very language needs to be reversed. Rather than talking about 'hearing loss', the term 'Deaf gain' could be used. What is it that we could gain by being or becoming deaf?[16]

Like the sociologist Dick Hebdige's articulation of youth subcultures as class-driven groups based around particular genres of music and fashion styles, the Deaf (sub)culture brings Deaf people together and allows them to express cultural and social subjectivities that they wouldn't be able to with hearing people.[17] It gives them freedom from the constant demands of conforming to normal hearing behavioural patterns. Here, speech and sound more generally is redundant to the operation of that culture.

In such environments, it is hearing people who would be disabled. Going to a Deaf dance club, for example, as a hearing person for the first time is an experience unlike any other. Vibrating floors, 'aroma DJs' (who mix smells that compliment the very bass-heavy music), intense video walls and sign dancers maximize the experience for Deaf people. Hearing people, who do not have the biological and/or social conditioning, simply are not easily able to process all the sensory data. These places are specifically a product of and for Deaf people, and would not exist without them.

More than creating new social spaces, Deaf people have augmented their own sensorial capacity. In the same way that Chris Downey found that in losing his sight, his sensory appreciation of the city was heightened, deafness can also augment other senses. There is increasing scientific evidence that indicates deaf people have improved peripheral vision. Studies of people born deaf have shown that their retinal neurons are more 'distributed' within the eye than those of people who can hear.[18] Specifically they are directed 'outward' toward the ears, in order to accommodate visual information from a broader field than directly in front. So, there is also a physiological difference in some deaf people that means they have subtly expanded visual fields.

Furthermore, neuroscientists studying brain activity in people born deaf have shown that they are often better at detecting motion and light in their peripheral vision than hearing people.[19] This is because the brain's plasticity adapts 'low-level' sensory 'real estate' that would otherwise be given over to hearing to be used by other senses. In other words, the brain of a deaf person has a better capacity to react to and process visual, haptic, gustatory or olfactory inputs. Deaf people, therefore, are hard-wired to experience the world differently.

Consequently, Deaf people are creating entirely new ways of experiencing a world that is undetectable to the 'hearing' population. People signing across a crowded noisy bar to each other, jokes and puns that only work in sign language, more attuned reactions to facial expressions and body language; these processes exemplify how Deaf people are creating very different ways of social interaction.

And of course, it is not just deafness that can bring about abilities to sense differently to what a normalized body can. Synaesthesia is a neurological condition in which sensorial perceptions are 'mixed' or alternate, so that synaesthetes (those with the condition) can see music or hear colour. Some synaesthetes have articulated how emotional stimulus and responses get mixed into the neurological pathways and so the blending of sensorial capacities can include emotions too.

Those who have synaesthesia are able to experience a world that is alien to people with 'normal' neurological sensorial capacities. Studies have been conducted that highlight how people with synaesthesia are more creative, and looking at the work of Jack Coulter it is easy to see why.[20] Coulter is a synaesthete who paints the colours he hears. In describing his form of synaesthesia, he has argued:

> If I feel emotionally stimulated within a specific situation, like staring at the sky or experiencing a sudden infatuation within a beautiful moment, my sight literally burns in fluorescence. That is an example of when my synaesthesia is stimulated within experiential form. The dominance lays [sic] within my ability to 'hear' colour, which is known as chromesthesia or sound-to-colour synaesthesia. I can vividly hear colours in prominence during the physical act of painting.[21]

The melding of emotion, visual form and sound creates a completely alien experience, one that to describe to a non-synaesthete would be like 'trying to describe what the world looks like to an individual who has been blind from birth'. Coulter's paintings are, of course, themselves consumable; they are for sale as prints, and his Instagram account has over 66,000 followers. The outputs therefore become commodified. But it is the experiences that Coulter has before putting brush to canvas that are 'creative' in the non-capitalist sense. He is experiencing stimuli that are simply not achievable by 'normal' sensibilities. The resultant works are vivid depictions of the world that he has access to: visual representations of a world that a non-synaesthete would never be able to experience.

And it's not just synaesthetes who can create artistic artefacts from different neurological capabilities. Trent Coffin is an illustrator who has suffered from Tourette's syndrome all his life. His 2013 film, *Phil the Phoenix*, depicts a young man named Phil, who periodically transmogrifies into a fiery phoenix and explodes, leaving his surroundings caked in ash. Coffin has been quoted online as saying that the film depicts his experiences of having Tourette's, so often reduced in popular culture to the 'swearing disease', and the butt of countless jokes. In the film, Phil's 'outbursts' are met with laughter, derision or sympathy.

Phil's teachers, his classmates, and even his parents wear grey suits with fire-resistant masks; they are shielding themselves from his Tourette's, refusing to expose themselves to the potential 'damage' it could do to their own bodies. These suits could be viewed as a metaphor for the majority's attempts to block out and subjugate any experiences it does not and cannot understand. In sum, by 'being normal', the majority put on suits that differentiate themselves as fully functioning, abled bodies; they are blocking the potential to empathize with this vastly different way of experiencing the world.

Then there is Neil Harbisson, a man born colour blind. He had a piece of light-sensing technology surgically implanted that allows him to hear colour via a microchip in the back of his head. Now Harbisson's perception of sound and colour are blurred, and he is able to make soundscapes of people's faces, and make paintings of pieces of music. Moreover, he has expanded the range of colours that he can hear beyond the normal range that the human eye can perceive. He can hear infrared and ultraviolet, so he can tell when someone is pointing a remote control at him, or when it is a particularly harmful day to sunbathe.[22] Harbisson created his 'hearing eye' as a result of colour blindness – a perceived defect in the normal functioning of the human body. The result is that he is able to experience the world in ways that those with 'normal' bodies cannot.

Normalization

Blindness, deafness, synaesthesia, Tourette's, colour-blindness-turned-extra-sensory (and many more besides): these 'minority' sensorial capacities provide experiences that the majority cannot directly perceive. The biological model of disability, with its focus on bringing all bodies in line with normality, seeks to converge these people's experiences of the sensorial world with those of the masses. And importantly for capitalist growth, normalizing the body makes it more likely to be able to perform creative labour efficiently without the need for expensive augmentation of the workplace.

In many countries, there is a deliberate policy of welfare and disability benefits geared toward making employable bodies.[23] In making deaf people hear and making blind people see there is an overt ideology of normalization. Such 'normalization' is, in many cases, a feat of fantastic medical ingenuity. Cochlear implants have given deaf people who want to be able to hear a chance to involve themselves in the hearing world, which for hearing parents of children born deaf (for example) is a highly advantageous and indeed joyous process. Also, older people who lose their hearing in later life can now have the opportunity to continue in their hearing world. These are modern-day medical miracles. But the joyousness of such occasions stems from a release from the grief process.

In other words, our contemporary societies, which champion competitiveness over compassion, market forces over cultural variation, labour over leisure and self-interest over sociality, reward the normal able body and marginalize and discriminate against the diffabled body, or anyone who cannot function efficiently as a capitalist worker. Being deaf, blind, mute, a wheelchair user, autistic, bipolar or any other of the myriad of alternative corporeal states within these societal parameters is indeed *dis*abling. Such people will inevitably suffer prejudice, discrimination and injustice from a social majority that is preoccupied with bringing all its subjects in line with the prevailing view of normality.

Hence, when someone does become 'normalized', it is a joyous occasion precisely because they will now have more potential advantages within mainstream capitalist society. In normalising bodies, capitalism is seductive: it offers the security that comes from the benefits it gives to that body.

But this normalization negates the experience of radically different subjectivities beyond the experience of capitalist 'normality'. It is very *un*creative. It is as if it clothes us all in the grey suits from Trent Coffin's film.

Such normalization processes are, however, rarely purely binary; the lure of capitalism to the majority may be strong, but it is not always a smooth path and rarely does it offer complete security. There will always be moments of further oppression, when the diffabled body will be all too aware of its marginality. Cochlear implants, for example, are not a complete 'cure' for deafness. They may allow people to grow up being able to speak, go to mainstream school and engage with hearing people day to day. But there are always moments of lack when the Deaf person butts up against the smooth functioning of the technologies of social and economic compliance. Music is often impossible to make out clearly, crowded environments are difficult to concentrate in (making schools and some workplaces particularly alienating places), lips still need to be read, regional accents can be like entirely different languages, and TV is a blur of sound that doesn't match the visuals.

As a result implanted people are not automatically part of hearing culture. They can find themselves 'in between cultures', not fully part of the established subculture of Deafness, but also not fully part of the hearing world either. Hence, there is a middle ground of existence. While this can be a real source of anxiety for many, it also offers the opportunity for the creation of an entirely new subculture. In the past few decades, as cochlear implants have become more prevalent, children are growing up with different modes of communication to those of Deaf and hearing people. Because of the way they learnt to 'hear', they exhibit very subtle differences in phonetics: for example 'd's and 'g's are often melded to create a phoneme that is unachievable for those able to speak 'normally'.[24] And they react to sound stimuli in very different ways.

There are charities, collectives and youth groups that cater specifically for cochlear implanted people and they are creating brand new modes of connectivity. Technologically driven, the emergence of a cochlear implant subculture 'in between' Deaf culture and the hearing world points to how diffabled people have the agency to create entirely new collective subjectivities (in this case, a subculture).

From these creative 'actualized' and shared experiences of diffabled people, ways that the world can progress beyond the neoliberal 'perfect self' can be glimpsed, utilized and acted upon in radical emancipatory, perhaps even anti-capitalist ways. But there is a need for everyone, especially those in the majority, to connect to these ways if we are to allow this creativity to flourish. Put bluntly, unless the majority connects, interacts and *empathizes* with diffabled people, new ways of experiencing the world are closed off before they are given a chance to proliferate. If we were in Trent Coffin's film, those of us who are not diffabled need to take off the grey suits.

First, there must be *access*, however brief or fleeting. This comes from being empathetic rather than simply being sympathetic. How can a hearing person really know what it is like to be deaf? How can someone 'of sane mind' really know what it is like to be schizophrenic? We can take advantage of all the medical technologies at our disposal to replicate the conditions, but these alternative experiences will never be directly perceived; they will be completely alien to the majority.

That is, of course, unless you're Joel Salinas, an American doctor from Boston. Salinas is a synaesthete, with the ability to feel someone else's pain by simply looking at them and/or touching them. His 'mirror touch' synaesthesia is multilayered: he looks upon the world as a 'multisensory landscape'.[25] The physical pain of a heart attack, the emotional pain of a grieving child, even death: Salinas details how his particular form of synaesthesia is both a blessing and a curse, but one that is beyond the comprehension of a large swath of the population, and in many cases, almost unbelievable.

However, Salinas's testimony suggests that his form of synaesthesia brings about a 'radical empathy', one that if replicated could put us 'inside the experiences of others and, in due process, allow an honest and authentic re-creation of their joy, their pain, their suffering, whatever they are experiencing, within ourselves.'[26] Not all of us have mirror touch synaesthesia. But the ability of non-diffabled people to be empathetic toward diffabled people – to understand, discuss, relate and *feel* with those of a different identity – is a fundamental part of engendering a more radical form of creativity. While Salinas's synaesthesia is indeed rare, the empathy he feels is a key part of a radical creativity that can connect people.

Salinas and the others discussed in this chapter have used their diffabilities to engage with capitalist processes, and even make money from them. This is of course a symptom of an all-pervasive capitalism that demands we surrender any 'new' ways of being to be monetized.

Those I have discussed in this chapter thus far will be the most 'visible' diffabled people, and hence those who have already engaged with (or been co-opted by) creative capitalism to some extent. Instagram followers, book sales, Ted Talk fees: these are all examples of how capitalism has seduced diffabled people into its own mechanisms of growth. But by looking to the visceral nature of their diffability as a means of critiquing the broader processes of co-option (even if they have fallen foul of it) there can be a broader realisation of an alterative, emancipatory form of creativity. Being radically empathetic in the way Salinas described is to connect with others, and go against the grain of the dogma of neoliberal creativity.

In so doing, othered experiences of sociality, camaraderie, solidarity and compassion come to fore that force at least a suspension from the rituals of self-interest, competition, monetization and introspection. Of course, everyday life includes too many instances in which this is not the case. Blind, deaf and other diffabled people are discriminated against in often-horrific ways. But by highlighting and championing the alternative modes of being-in-the-world that diffability affords, and crucially getting more people, institutions and even governments to connect with and understand it, a more radical and progressive creativity can be realized.

But that danger of co-option is always there: capitalism's 'creative' appropriation mechanisms are so efficient that there is always a risk that by celebrating diffabled experiences, they can be monetized in some way. In March 2016, a new advertising campaign by Smirnoff Vodka was launched which depicted deaf dancers, under the tagline 'We're open.' The depiction of deaf people dancing to silence is a destabilization of 'normal' ways of behaving (albeit perhaps a very minor tremor). People dance-signing to silence may be an image that goes against mainstream views of dancing, but when the music in the video crescendos, and the usual motifs of contemporary consumer capitalism hit the screen, one cannot help but feel that there has been a crass co-option of this unique subculture.

What is more, using the tagline 'We're open' speaks to the articulation of tolerance as a quality that corporations need to espouse to compete. This draws on Florida's creative class theory. With the specific import of tolerance as a quality that spurs economic growth, corporations are quick to display openness to diversity, including diffability.

This, on the surface, is a positive action. For example in March 2016, Disney threatened to boycott filming in the US state of Georgia if it passed controversial anti-gay legislation. A month later Bruce Springsteen and Bryan Adams, two global rock superstars, cancelled gigs in North Carolina and Mississippi respectively because of anti-LGBT laws being passed in those US states. Such actions are important steps in showing that society, even large corporations, will not tolerate such bigotry. However, such actions belie the broader co-optive force of capitalism and its use of 'tolerance' as a means of generating further growth and a swelling of the centre at the expense of the margins.

Multinational corporations may preach tolerance (usually in a Global North setting) on the one hand, but continue to exploit labour, suppress wages, and espouse hyper-masculinized, white and able-bodied aesthetics on the other. So they are often guilty of Orwellian double-speak.

Creativity, as it is currently defined, pays lip service to these marginal identities (diffabled, queer or otherwise) as mere fuel for diversity; they are presented as evidence of a heterogeneous and multicultural society, and are therefore the foundations for the influx of the creative class and all the subsequent injustices that entails, including, ironically, the continued oppression of diffabled people. But foundations are stable. By being radically creative in seeking out diffabled or minority ways of being, we can start to shake those foundations; the normalized identities of a white, able-bodied, and male creative class suddenly become very unstable. It is in this instability that new things can form; it is in this instability that we find the most creative people.

Chris Downey, the blind architect, has said that there are two types of people in the world. There are those with disabilities, and those who haven't found theirs yet.[27] To be truly creative then is to find that disability and explore how it changes your world.

3

Politics: Austere Creativity

In 2001 in the UK, the band Hear'Say released their debut song, 'Pure and Simple'. It became the best-selling debut single of all time, and their accompanying album also went straight in at number one on the UK album charts. The band had not spent years on the club circuit, honing their skills in front of tiny crowds in the back rooms of pubs. They hadn't been in and out of record company executive offices being turned down time after time. Hear'Say did not take years to become an overnight sensation: they took about six weeks. This is because they were the subject of a brand-new UK television show, one of the first reality TV shows based on a 'creative' art form.

While the late 1990s saw New Labour implementing its creative industries strategy, a reality TV phenomenon was emanating from a small Auckland-based television production company called Screentime. In 1999, they produced a show called *Popstars*. It mapped out the lives of members of the public auditioning to be in a pop group created specifically for the show by real life record executives. People queued up, sang in front of a panel of stern judges, and over the course of the series, were whittled down to just five. They went on to form a new pop group and were unleashed into the music charts. The show was an instant hit.

The format was so successful that it was sold to media conglomerates all over the world, including the UK and the US. The show debuted in the UK in February 2001 and six weeks later Hear'Say, a group of five twentysomethings that included a youth worker, a receptionist, and a backing vocalist, rocketed to pop superstardom.

Soon after, it spawned hundreds of similar formats all over the world, all aping the general-public-to-pop-star format: *Pop Idol*, *The X Factor*, *The Voice* and many more besides. The concept has been replicated across other forms of creative practice including cake baking, ballroom dancing, cooking and landscape painting. The twenty-first century has seen our TV screens saturated with the reality TV talent show format, a format that comprises a panel of in-studio judges and audience voting systems. Any new big budget Saturday night entertainment television programme now will no doubt contain an element of judging, audience selection via real-time voting, and the tension of announcing a 'winner'.

The worldwide uptake of this format has driven the proliferation of a version of creativity that seems utterly devoid of content. Its narratives – uncovering hidden creativity and rags to riches – riff on the belief that 'anyone can make it'. It is the mediatized and spectacularized version of the emancipation of enterprising self. If you wanted to be a pop star, now you had the pathway to achieve this. If you have the talent, you can make it. What's more, it is a far more democratic process, with the viewing public ultimately responsible for the 'winner'.

These TV shows have provided an intoxicating mix of staged democracy and an underdog story of the ordinary citizen becoming a superstar, set within a melodrama of pantomime villains, fairy godmothers and public scrutiny. Their success forms part of a broader 'universe' of reality TV shows, starting with the globally successful *Big Brother* created by the Dutch TV company Endemol in 1999. It was not based on finding personal creative talent or innate 'star' quality. Instead, *Big Brother* (and its more contemporary cousins such as *Gogglebox*, *I'm a Celebrity ...*, *Love Island* and the endless number of copycats) normalizes and indeed carnivalizes round-the-clock surveillance and subservience to a hidden but omnipotent force. The voyeurism in these shows is more explicit than it is in the glorified karaoke shows, but no less exploitative. Put these forms of reality TV together and we have a potent mix that has allowed for the subtle, but very real advancement of the ideologies of self-promotion, hyper-mediation and deep surveillance further into the routine of creative media production and consumption.

Of course, this phenomenon has not gone unnoticed by the political class. The onset of the creative industries and the new obsession with reality TV as a quick and easily-replicable way of producing 'creative' content found favour with a political class clamouring for airtime and attention in the increasingly crowded media landscape. So politicians and their spin doctors, with the lobbyists and genuflecting sycophants behind them, began to take advantage of this new manifestation of creativity to radically reframe how political power was wielded.

In 2015 and 2016, as the US presidential race heated up, the Republican Party staged a series of debates across America between its candidates. The first, held in August 2015, had ten candidates jostling for position on stage on the US TV network Fox News. The last debate was in March 2016, and by then those ten had been whittled down to only four. By May 2016, the one man left standing after the 'voting public' had decided was Donald Trump.

Ever since the media-savvy and supremely confident JFK triumphed over Richard Nixon in the first televised United States presidential debate in 1960, US politics has embraced the means of media manipulation to win elections. TV debates between Republican candidates have been a staple of US politics since the '60s, but they have become increasingly stylized over the years, not only in the slick presentation by the networks, but also in the way the candidates conduct themselves on stage. Responding to the anchor's questions, addressing the audience in the room but also the millions watching, the subtle (and not-so-subtle) attacks on their competitors: these debates look and feel like the reality TV shows that saturate our screens (often, due to scheduling chicanery, immediately before or after the debates). Indeed, they are designed to do so. The television executives, whose jobs are dependent upon ratings, ratchet up the 'wow' factor by pandering to the fad for stylized, auditoria-filled and theatre-like staging. And the politicians behave in a way that mirrors the celebrities and personas of these reality TV programmes.

Trump has finessed this persona. He comes from one of the most successful reality TV formats, *The Apprentice*. Hence he is all too familiar with the intense stage management of reality TV, having been involved in the production of the show from the outset. He was able to seamlessly segue into the political debate format, spouting cutting sound bites that became sloganized, disregarding and deliberately simplifying political complexities, and commanding the stage with complete disregard for the anchor's authority.[1] He revelled in the celebrity and surveillance culture that reality TV had normalized, and, with a little help from social media, transposed it to the most powerful office in the world. Like reality TV, with its acquiescence to an *unreal* reality, US presidential debates have lost any connection to political realties with all their contradictions, complexities and real-life consequences. They have taken on a form of creative industrial production in which the constructed reality is far more packageable and profitable than real life.

But the politics of real life have been hollowed out by a system that foregrounds spectacular creative-industry-aping politics, champions style over political substance, and suppresses (and eventually completely conceals) political nuance. In a complete role reversal, this hyper-mediated and stylized creative industry has made the contingent and complex reality of everyday politics completely *unreal*.

Beyond the US, televised debates are now a permanent feature of national campaigns in many countries; they too have succumbed to the resulting suppression of reality. Political campaigning is no longer about real issues. It is the ability of candidates to impress within the confines of a highly manicured media circus that is scrutinized by the mainstream and social media commentariat. Politicians are put in front of the cameras and probed on their ability to answer questions truthfully, but without any acknowledgement about how that truth manifests in real life. They are judged on their ability to recount numbers, avoid platitudes and deflect direct attacks; and it is all rated in real-time by social media. Much like the discussion shows after reality TV shows, post-debate segments pore over every sentence.[2]

Rather than clarifying the political nuances that a debate may have obscured, the very existence of these post-debate segments renders the debate more 'unreal'. 'Spin rooms' are set up where an army of sycophants attempt to ossify their leaders' narrative to a media baying for sound bites, controversy and/or potential gaffes. The debate is treated like a TV show, a drama whose plot holes should be unpicked. All this then comes to a head when the audience, or a focus group, make their choice at the ballot box. It plays out like one large reality TV show: winners, losers, hard-luck stories, harsh judges and ultimately, a chance to influence the result.

Lacanian psychoanalysis contends that there is a fundamental difference between the Real and the constructed reality, with the latter being purposefully constructed to obscure the former. Sometimes, however, the Real can bring reality crashing down and expose the deficiencies and injustices of the systems of control.[3] But the Real can be glimpsed only as it 'ruptures' that constructed reality; too much exposure risks the carefully contrived reality being destroyed. Hence capitalism's desire to continuously strive for the smooth functioning of its own reality involves the everyday suppression of the Real. As a result, the *real* politics is hidden from us behind the performance of political drama.

To compound this further, we get 'actual' political dramas as creative media that satirize but then end up pre-empting real-life political decisions and behaviour. TV shows such as *The Thick of It* and *House of Cards* lay out seemingly absurd political situations, only to have actual politicians perform them for real at a later date. In the modern US version of *House of Cards*, this unreal reality is played out most forcefully when Frank Underwood (the president character) breaks the fourth wall by talking directly into the camera to us, the viewing audience. In a particularly telling scene when he is on trial, he looks into the camera and says:

> In the end, I don't care whether you love me or you hate me, just as long as I win.
>
> The deck is stacked. The rules are rigged.
>
> Welcome to the death of the Age of Reason.

There is no right or wrong. Not anymore. There's only being in …
    and then being out.[4]

In a direct critique of Trump and the division his administration stokes, the show has become part of the veneer of
political reality. The 'death of the Age of Reason' line in
particular can be seen as a reference to the constant attacks
by Trump and his administration on the mass media, painting their objective fact-telling narratives as 'fake news'.

Creative media and shows such as *House of Cards* become
complicit in the political landscape and its arguments and
counter-arguments. These shows begin to perform our
politics for us. After all, the shows we watch and the people
we follow on social media are advertised across our online
virtual selves. It does not take much time at all to peruse
someone's Facebook or Twitter feed to discover who they
vote for, which politicians they like and dislike and which
political narratives they most closely align themselves with.
Hence, political persuasion (and activity) becomes another
badge, another artefact to aid in curating the online self. It
becomes a means to an end – that end being rooted in a constant need for self-promotion that neoliberalism demands
at all times.

This was described by the sociologist Erving Goffman,
who wrote in 1956 about the presentation of the self in
everyday life. Goffman's work was highly prescient of the
mediated world of the twenty-first century when he argued
that within the profusion of social situations, people played
different roles in a 'multistage drama'. Therefore actors

change their persona depending on who or what they were interacting with.[5]

Reality TV, and the creative enmeshing of politics and media, introduced a hyper-construction of the self, with those on screen (reality TV celebrity or politician) now carefully portraying the 'right' personality in order to 'win' over the viewing public.[6] The ironic consequence of this is that the reality of 'reality TV' has been lost: it has become mediated into a hyper-virtuality of pervasive online communication and politics, endless programming and constant bombardment of stylized and manicured imagery.

And with the advent of social media, this has been exacerbated, allowing people to curate online content to represent a particular brand of the virtual self; and in Trump's case use it to communicate actual governmental policy.[7] The 'backstage' reality (that Goffman alluded to as the more 'real' version of the self) and the Lacanian Real are now totally hidden from view, and consigned to the very *un*reality of non-mediated, often offline physical space. Party politics has become part of the wider consumption cycle of capitalism, and dismisses the Real in favour of a constructed capitalist realism.[8]

When detailing the Society of the Spectacle in 1967, Guy Debord argued that:

> Celebrities figure various styles of life and various views of society which anyone is supposedly free to embrace and pursue in a global manner. Themselves incarnations of the inaccessible results of

social labour, they mimic by-products of that labour, and project these above labour so that they appear as its goal. The by-products in question are power and leisure — the power to decide and the leisure to consume which are the alpha and the omega of a process that is never questioned. In the former case, government power assumes the personified form of the pseudostar; in the second, stars of consumption canvas for votes as pseudopower over life lived. But, just as none of these celestial activities are truly global, neither do they offer any real choices.[9]

The characteristics of twenty-first century populist creative politicking embody much of this dualism between the 'pseudo-star' of government and the 'pseudo-power' of celebrity. It blends the creativity that is required to conjure a virtual celebrity persona with the political creativity of winning votes. The two realms have collided into a single realm of political creative consumption, where government leaders masquerade as celebrities of the cultural realm, and celebrities interject into political discourse.

With social media, blogging and the relentless desire for online 'op-eds' and 'hot takes', political commentators have taken on celebrity status, and anyone with a healthy Twitter follower count can be a vaunted voice in political debate. Comedians, musicians, film stars, retired sports persons, TV talk-show hosts and others have become mouthpieces of political ideologies of various hues, while politicians embrace social media, op-eds, cultural outlets, popular TV shows, radio shows, concerts and, indeed, concert-style rallies to spread their messages.

The fog of sociopolitical media enshrines and permeates our everyday lives but, as Debord noted half a century ago, these 'celestial' activities are not global in their representation of the political.[10] In other words, they do not account for the nuanced and actual experience of everyday politics. Nor do they represent anything other than a replication of the constructed reality of the status quo. Instead, the political commentariat 'performs' in the broader sociopolitical landscape as the bogeymen lying in wait if you stray too far from the safe space of normalized thought, scaring you back into the quotidian rhythms of capitalist life.

The daily dance of these extreme political views plays out on Twitter feeds, radio phone-ins, the comment sections of blogs and the rolling tickertapes across twenty-four-hour news outlets. Indeed, the army of bots on Twitter (for example) are mass-produced to flood these with extreme political (both left- and right-wing) opprobrium in an attempt to influence society and even determine political outcomes.[11] Everything is now 'politicized'. The very public and often vitriolic confrontations that spring from this foster introspection, a lack of discussion and/or consensual thinking and a reliance on algorithmic pathways of visibility. What becomes important is how many likes you get, or how quickly your idea reverberates around the echo-chamber Facebook has created for you.[12]

Furthermore, 'creativity' plays a central role in gaining that audience. To be visible is to engage in the capitalist mode of creativity and entrepreneurialism. It is the process of branding the self, cultivating instantaneous appeal, remaining flexible at all times. It is to willingly feed the continual construction of a neoliberal reality, one that conceals the political Real of mass inequality, precariousness and institutional prejudice, or repackages it in order to serve the inflation of the self. But these are very 'real' political problems that are either being ignored, or subsumed into the hyper-mediated creative political landscape as simply another item on the news agenda that can generate debate, and therefore clicks, and therefore likes, and therefore eyeballs, and therefore profit.

But this Real contains people whose lives are being completely destroyed. It is an arena that remains 'outside' the mainstream political and creative media-inspired commentariat spaces, but one that is a direct consequence of it. Because it is a Real that has been hugely affected by one of the most damaging political, and indeed, 'creative' ideologies of our time – austerity.

Creativity and Austerity

The onset of the financial crisis in 2008 should have signalled the first major crisis for neoliberalism.[13] It was anything but. The crisis, which caused recessions all over the world, was itself a product of a process that the creativity narrative has championed relentlessly, namely financial innovation. The crash is widely recognized to have started with the subprime mortgage crisis in the US. Along with payday loans, extended credit lines and other high-interest financial technologies that locked vulnerable people into long-term indebtedness, subprime mortgages were 'innovations' that came from the financial services sector engaging in 'creative' practices.[14] With these high-interest mortgages, banks lent vast amounts of money to 'subprime' people, those who had been refused credit elsewhere and had no financial ability to realistically pay that money back in the agreed term.

This build-up of household debt led to an enormous number of people defaulting on their payments. The housing market dived and ultimately the banks could not shift the toxic debt. Many of the major banks in the US filed for bankruptcy, the biggest being Lehman Brothers in September 2008. Given the globally hyper-connected financial industrial landscape, once large international banks begin to collapse on one side of the Atlantic, it is inevitable that banks and other financial institutions in Europe, Asia and then the Global South would do the same. Deep national recessions were the result, with unemployment, wage depression and increased poverty on unprecedented scales.

The onset of the crisis was the first major test of the resilience of these financialized policies. Rather than spelling their demise, though, the aftermath of the financial crisis has ushered in further development of financial and competitive logics upon everyday life in the form of austerity. In both the US and UK a number of banks were bailed out by the national governments. Those who supported the bailouts argued that the injection of public money was needed to stop the financial crisis from deepening, as further bank collapses might spread yet further misery. Some banks were heralded as 'too big to fail'. It has been calculated that globally, US$3.6 trillion, 5.73 per cent of global gross domestic product, was handed out to the banks by national governments between 2007 and 2008.[15]

The action was necessary to secure the post-recessionary 'success' of the neoliberal project.[16] Rhetorically, the narrative of the bailouts was of 'getting the banks lending again'. Therefore, the political language was one entirely of economic rationality.[17] The then Labour Prime Minister of the UK, Gordon Brown, said in 2008, 'This support [the £500 billion bailout of the UK banks] is on commercial terms. We expect to be rewarded for the support we provide.'[18]

The decision was supported by the majority of the government and its opposition. The UK led the way in the bailouts, and many European countries soon followed suit. The bailouts were cast as an investment strategy first and foremost; moreover, they allowed a further weapon of capitalist expansion to be wielded without credible political opposition – namely austerity.

The rationale for this round of austerity was always one of 'balancing the national books' and making the UK more competitive in the 'global race'.[19] But austerity politics in the UK is an ideology that has catalysed structural changes in public spending, such as the net reduction of funds for the NHS, leading to the influx of privatization schemes. It has also meant reductions in welfare, wage caps on public sector pay, reduction in local council funding, and the 'streamlining' of regulatory bodies.

In the EU more broadly, austerity has brought about a

reduction in pensions, longer working hours and cuts to the level of the minimum wage.[20] In the US, it meant even further devolvement of social welfare to state government, cuts to homeless shelters and to denying poor children breakfast at school.[21] But austerity is not based in economic rationality; nor is there any sense that it is a progressive means of welfare provision (indeed, it has been widely debunked).[22] It is an ideological project aimed at changing the very nature of the socioeconomic realm.

In general terms, austerity is the reduction of expenditure to decrease debt, be that personal, within a household, or a national government's. The rhetoric of creativity bubbles under the surface of much of the programme. Goods and services under the control of the state are sold off to private contractors under the assumption that private companies are more innovative and efficient as they operate under the rubric of market logic. Public sector workers have their pay capped and are told that they can 'do more with less' if they engage in creative (often digital or 'sharing economy') practices. Public institutions are told to turn to 'grassroots' creative schemes to underpin local services that have seen their funding drastically reduced.

This was particularly acute in the case of libraries, museums and other repositories of public knowledge, which up to this moment had been pivotal in the transformation of the rhetoric of creativity. Since the 1990s they had been icons of urban redevelopment, largely thanks to the 'success' of creative and culture-led regeneration's patient zero: the Guggenheim Museum in Bilbao.[23] But more than simply stimulating gentrification with palatable flagship projects, they became vehicles for the corporatisation of culture and the privatization of public knowledge.

The policy landscape of the creative industries around the turn of the century in Europe, Australia (and to a lesser extent, the US) leveraged public institutions as bait for inward investment in the new knowledge-based economy. After all, the creative class theory stated that creative and talented people were attracted to places that had the right mix of cultural lifestyle, nightlife and diversity. Museums, galleries and modern libraries had the right mix of intellectualism, cultural diversity and old school charm to woo these footloose, agile and energetic creative types. So when these institutions' funding was reduced via austerity measures, they had to look to sponsorship deals and philanthropists to plug the funding gaps.

The larger institutions in global cities were able to adjust to the changing winds of investment strategies with some large-scale (and ethically questionable) sponsorship arrangements. For instance in 1996, BP began sponsoring the British Museum, and it has also recently signed a five-year deal to sponsor the National Portrait Gallery, Royal Opera House and the Royal Shakespeare Company. BP also had a long-running sponsorship deal with the Tate London, which only ended after twenty-six years because of climate change activists who continually campaigned in and around the gallery.[24] Despite receiving large state subsidies these institutions engaged in corporate activities to bolster their profitability, and to maintain a competitive edge over other institutions and other cities in the country and globally.

But the mix of corporate funding on the one hand and a reduction in public funding on the other has two problematic effects for 'smaller' cultural institutions.[25] The overwhelming majority of arts funding in the UK occurs in London – 40 per cent in 2014 – a clear indication of a metropolitan bias.[26] Furthermore, the austerity programme led to a 40 per cent reduction in local council budgets after 2015. Many small-scale, localized and community focused public cultural assets were systematically reduced.

For example, libraries have had their funding cut by £25 million in 2015/6 (a drop of 2.6 per cent) and the number of libraries open has reached a ten-year low.[27] Many libraries now have to change their remit to be 'community hubs' and offer social services such as outreach events, children's education and mental health programmes for pensioners.[28] The evolution of libraries into more community-orientated centres is a welcome augmentation of prized public assets, particularly in the face of the digitization of resources. But being forced into this change because of a lack of alternative social services and community centres creates an environment of enforced entrepreneurialism and corporatization. One library has even started to rent out its free desk space to freelancers for a small fee, an act that finally and completely monetizes the very 'public' act of libraries offering free workspace for all.[29]

Libraries and other public institutions have traditionally been repositories of collective and civic knowledge, and archives of local cultures and histories. But they have become drawn into the creativity rhetoric by virtue of their subject matter. They have been forced to compete in the new global landscape of creative industrial activity because they are traditional places of knowledge rather than because they are designed to be competitive and commercial. This in turn brings with it the myriad of problems and inequalities that this version of creativity fuels: massive regional disparities, with investment focused on larger metropolitan regions at the expense of their hinterlands; the removal of services and activities that cater for the underprivileged and marginal; the destruction of public assets with deep local histories; and, inevitably, the privatization of social services.

Austerity has been implemented, forcing these institutions to be more 'creative'. It has recast public cultural institutions as panaceas of this new austere world. Libraries can diversify to be social service centres; museums can hold evening classes; leisure centres can host school PE lessons. But it has primed them for appropriation because their ability to act as engines of non-capitalist knowledge and social practices has been eroded and, in some cases, completely destroyed, only for them to be resurrected as another agent of capitalist, competitive and entrepreneurial versions of creativity.

In the face of severe reductions in funding from national government, local councils in the UK have been forced to turn to citizen- and volunteer-run programmes to deliver social and public services. In 2010, the then prime minister,

David Cameron, announced his plans to introduce the 'Big Society'. In the speech he gave to launch it, he described the Big Society as a culture

> where people, in their everyday lives, in their homes, in their neigh-
> bourhoods, in their workplace, don't always turn to officials, local
> authorities or central government for answers to the problems they
> face, but instead feel both free and powerful enough to help them-
> selves and their own communities.[30]

So when local civic groups or volunteers step in to run a library that has had its budget fatally cut, it is rebranded as 'community creativity', plugging the gaps left by a neces- sary programme of 'living within our means'. While the level of enthusiasm and engagement of local communities should be applauded, the broader ideology of utilising these resources to prop up the austerity programme should not. It is part of the structural problems of this version of creativity. The collective energies and resources used up in replicat- ing public services *could* be directed toward alternative programmes of social provision that run counter to capi- talism's injustices, but under austerity, they are utilized to *re*produce what already existed (albeit perhaps with a local 'twist'). It maintains the status quo. Austerity and creativity go hand-in-glove in crushing any alternative to capitalist society. And post-2008's financial crash, the implementation of austerity has only intensified.

Austerity has turbocharged inequality. It has had a hugely negative impact on welfare provision, particularly unemployment and disability benefits. It has reduced real wages for public sector workers such as nurses, teachers, firefighters and others. The narrative from governments has been one of 'rewarding hard-working families': espousing the now-familiar tropes of encouraging self-interest, entrepreneurialism and risk-taking by removing social welfare.

Again, this chimes with the mantra of 'creative work': labourers are forced to do 'more with less' or, in other words, work far beyond their paid working hours.

For example, in 2005, the Labour government introduced the Work Capability Assessment (WCA), a regular test that all those claiming benefit for being unemployed (whether registered disabled or not) had to undertake. If the test proved that the claimant was 'fit for work' then parts of that benefit would be revoked. The assessors were not a government agency, but a private IT company, Atos. The company received a fee for each assessment, and were given further incentives for passing people fit to work.

Hence, it was in Atos's best interest to pass as many people as possible, regardless of whether they were fit for work or not. Couple this with cuts to the baseline benefit payment levels and disability allowances, and the WCA system has created an environment in which people are financially disadvantaged for not being able to work even if their disability prevents them from doing so.

In March 2013, Michael O'Sullivan, a man who suffered from chronic depression and agoraphobia, was passed 'fit for work'. Six months later he killed himself. The coroner's report, released in 2015, gave a damning indictment of the process, stating that the 'trigger' for O'Sullivan's suicide had been the decision to pass him 'fit for work'.³¹ Moreover, the report found that Atos, on behalf of the WCA, failed to ask appropriate questions, spot signs of serious depressive thoughts and disregarded O'Sullivan's mental health issues as a serious barrier to being employed. Despite the evidence of three GPs to the contrary, O'Sullivan was continually assessed as 'fit to work' by Atos staff.

It wasn't just O'Sullivan: an extensive academic study found that from 2010 to 2013, there were 590 suicides as a result of the assessment process, and a vast rise in the number of people suffering mental illness as a direct consequence of the stress induced by being systematically and continually assessed by the government.³² This is the coalface of austerity in the UK: the mix of outsourcing government decision-making to for-profit companies, those companies putting their profit margins ahead of claimants' welfare, and the deliberate reduction in financial support for marginalized peoples. It is repeated in health (with the creeping privatization of the NHS), 'contracted-out prisons', private police forces and other public services.

In 2013, Raquel Rolnik, a United Nations special rapporteur for housing, visited the UK at the government's invitation to conduct a review into the UK's adherence to an international human rights standard. The 'bedroom tax' or, to give it its official title, the 'Removal of the Spare Room Subsidy' had just been introduced: it reduced housing benefit for those households with 'spare bedrooms'.³³ Rolnik's report was damning. It said that many people affected by the implementation of the bedroom tax were in 'tremendous despair'.[34]

Cuts to housing benefit, including the introduction of the bedroom tax and the cancellation of benefit for eighteen- to twenty-one-year-olds, have been another vehicle for austerity in the UK. Other international agencies have identified that since 2014, the UK has 'flat-lined' on key measures of social progress, and risks slipping backwards if austerity measures are not reversed.[35] It is clear then that austerity has no economic or social reasoning. It is an ideological project, one that is fundamentally altering the role of the state from one of welfare provision, public service and regulation, to one of enabling the 'creative' appropriation by capitalism of all vestiges of social life from which profit can be squeezed.

Austerity is not restricted to the UK and it forms part of the broader remit of the European Union, an institution that itself is complicit with the implementation of neoliberalism across the continent.[36] The recessions caused by the financial crisis across Europe were severe. Many countries – Portugal, Ireland, Greece, Cyprus, Romania, Latvia, Hungary and Spain – received large bailouts from the European Central Bank. In Greece's case, its debt levels were so high that the EU has imposed no fewer than fourteen austerity packages (so far – the latest was in May 2017). Not even the left-leaning Syriza government and a national referendum in 2015 that overwhelmingly rejected the terms of (one of the) EU's bailout packages was able to halt the imposition of massive austerity within Greece.[37]

In the US, austerity was even harsher. An IMF report concluded that between 2010 and 2013, the US reduced spending by 4.9 per cent of GDP; in the UK, it was 3.7 per cent, and in Spain, 4.2 per cent.[38] As a result, there were an estimated 4,750 'excess' suicides in the US, and an increase in problems of drug usage linked to the rise in unemployment.[39]

There has also been a huge rise in the suicide rate in Japan and many European countries.[40] All over the world, austerity programmes have forced citizens to be more 'creative', but in so doing, they have imprinted a neoliberal ideology further into the social fabric. Too often, with deadly results.

Creative Regulation

On 30 April 2014, Kareem Serageldin was sentenced to thirty months in prison in the US for the crime of 'fraudulently inflating the prices of asset-backed bonds which comprised subprime residential mortgage backed securities and commercial mortgage backed securities in Credit Suisse's trading book in late 2007 and early 2008'.[41] He remains the only person to be prosecuted as a direct result of the subprime mortgage scandal that sparked the global recession. The fact that the financial elites avoided prosecution is a major point of contention in the protests against austerity measures and financial power more broadly. The reward for crashing the global economy was trillion-dollar bailouts; the reward for the poor was austerity.

Moreover, this political decision was cast as a *natural*

reaction to a crisis propagated by the greedy actions of the elite few: a triumph for the capitalist versions of creativity. The decade before the crash creativity was infused into economic rationality, and heralded as an essential characteristic for any industry, firm or institution. The creative class were lauded as the golden geese of growth. Meanwhile institutions both public and private were adjusting their physical and managerial architectures to capture and cater for the new lifeblood of the economy, creativity.

This involved attacking the regulations that were perceived to be blockages to unleashing creativity. Post-2008, much of the regulatory control designed to stop the 'casino banking' that caused the crash was lambasted as being too weak and insipid, even by the banking industry itself. Yet despite the full resources of the state, with its regulatory powers, law enforcement, justice system and vested public interest, Serageldin remains the only banker to be jailed, and many of the regulations have not been tightened. Rather than blaming individuals and bringing them to justice, it was the system that was at fault, it was regulation that had straightjacketed creativity, and hence it must be removed by the state.

This 'naturalization' of creativity into government was always part of the script. For example, Richard Florida borrows a rather ugly term from Jane Jacobs to describe those political institutions that impede the economic capacity of the creative class, 'squelchers'. These are 'overly controlling types who believe that they and they alone know what's best for their city or region.'[42] Urban governments that asked Florida to wear a suit and tie when he came to give his talks, and downplay the importance of bohemians and gays to economic growth are squelchers. People who criticize and are trapped by their pasts are squelchers. Florida has argued that squelchers are people who say 'no' a lot to new ideas simply because they are new. Essentially, if you or your institution stands in the way of creativity, you are a squelcher and need to move aside.

Florida is particularly vitriolic toward cities that build sports stadia to attract NFL franchises.[43] He sees them as 'squelching' the uptake of the creative class to a particular city. These stadia are used infrequently throughout the year, create mainly service class jobs that are low paid and contribute very little to the local economy. He has argued that they take public taxpayers' money which, via undemocratic local government processes, ends up lining the pockets of billionaire NFL franchise owners. In one op-ed on the issue, he proclaims:

> It's time to put an end to runaway public subsidies to lucrative sports franchises. Is there any other industry or field of business where taxpayers are asked to hand over astronomical sums to billionaire owners and their millionaire employees?[44]

A valid question no doubt. However, Florida has been very vocal on Twitter and other online media more recently about how to attract Amazon's second headquarters to a particular city.[45] Amazon announced to great fanfare in September 2017 that it was to build HQ2, it's second 'home' in another city outside Seattle, where its main headquarters are, asking for cities to bid for the right to house it. He has corralled his home city of Toronto (among others) to bid for HQ2. Notwithstanding the precariousness embedded in Amazon's employment models, any city bidding for HQ2 will undoubtedly ensure that public subsidies are handed over to the company's billionaire owner in the same way as they do with sports stadia. Presumably it is more acceptable in this case because Amazon is a tech company.

Sports stadia may indeed create fewer jobs than Amazon headquarters, but many Americans actually quite enjoy watching NFL games. To dismiss the regulatory urban frameworks that decide these things as 'squelching' creativity is evidence of an extremely one-dimensional view of what creativity is: one purely dependent upon how much money it can generate for a city. The economic rationality for *not* building a sports stadium may well be convincing in terms of jobs creation, multiplier effects and quality of life for the creative class a city is looking to attract, but in deriding such actions as 'squelching' creativity further entrenches the dogma of the creative narrative as the only way of societal progress, economically or otherwise.

Needless to say, these squelching voices were silenced post-2008. In the aftermath of the crash, it was surmised that the productive and economic-growth-stimulating creativity so prized in the creative class could aid in national and even global recovery. It just now had to be rolled out to every citizen in society; every job had to be 'creatified'. Doing less with more, being creative, being austere: under a capitalist discourse so ubiquitous, these were the only 'natural' reaction to the global recession.

A/political Creativity?

The dismissal of political practices that do not foreground 'creativity' as the only means by which we can make progress as a society is now accepted across the political spectrum. This is precisely because it has, over time, been moulded into a seemingly non-political, or post-political, character-istic. Indeed, who *doesn't* want to be seen as creative?

But when the context to the question is one of a class-based project of austerity, it becomes a far more pertinent one. The broad appeal of creativity, and its apparent political neutrality, has emptied the term of any non- or anti-capitalist politics and ethics. Austerity and governmen-tal implementation of the 'creative' mind set have rendered any subversive or resistive creativity as going against the 'natural' order to societal progress. It has been cast as illiberal. The lengths to which observers insist on the apo-liticality of creativity show how forcefully it is being used as a means to impose the 'political neutrality' of capitalist growth. Take this diatribe from Florida:

> I'm middle-aged, white, Italian-American, married, and straight. I have voted for and served under Democrats, Republicans, and inde-pendents, and I work closely with mayors, governors, and business, political and civic leaders from both sides of the aisle on economic development issues. The members of my core team of colleagues

and collaborators include Canadian, Swedish, and other international researchers, as well as Americans, registered Democrats and Republicans, far left socialists, staunch conservatives, liberal and libertarians, married and single people who are both straight and gay, recent college graduates and the middle-aged. What binds us together is not a political agenda but our common determination to identify the factors that drive economic development and the standard of living.[46]

Florida is claiming that the essential values of his theory of creativity are above and beyond party politics, gender, sexuality and nationality. Indeed the broad popularized appeal of the creative class, creative city and creative industry arguments is *cross*-political. On one hand it is prized as an important part of socially just, progressive, left-leaning politics. On the other extreme, those on the right of the political spectrum have welcomed the injection of creativity into mainstream political discourse because of its intimate ties to the spread of neoliberal ideologies and the reduction of regulation.

But creativity is never, and nor should it be, *a*political. To argue that economic development and standards of living for society are not driven by a political, or indeed ideological, agenda is to miss the point entirely. Capitalism's creative mechanisms of appropriation drive economic development, and any party's political interventionist programme will serve only to continue this because it is now the *only* way for it to be so.

Despite this, there are many initiatives and collectives

that are creative in direct opposition to capitalism's growth, and the austerity it wields. In Greece, years of 'fiscal discipline' imposed by the EU have led to massive cuts in social services, health, pensions and welfare provisioning. All the while the migration crisis has seen an influx of refugees and asylum seekers from the Middle East fleeing to Europe, with Greece often being their first port of call. This has led to vast urban populations (notably in Athens) of marginalized people struggling to acquire the basic means of survival.

In response to this, local activist and anarchist groups have set up 'urban solidarity spaces' that tackle the social reproduction of austerity, bring in marginalized people, and resist the xenophobic tendencies inherent in the public sphere in Athens.[47] They have set up 'time banks', which mediate the exchange of goods and services among participants (locals and refugees) based on time spent rather than monetary value. This allows social services to be offered directly to those in need and fosters a mutualism among those most affected by austerity.

The creation of local and alternative forms of exchange value is gaining popularity in various parts of the globe because of their direct resistance to capitalism's focus on money, but also because of their inclusivity; they allow those who have been excluded from capitalism's riches via austerity to be included in the community's riches instead. Local currencies such as the Brixton Pound in the UK, the Tumin in Epsinal, Mexico, and the purely digital currency of Tems in Volos in Greece have been used to encourage solidarity between local participants.

There are even experiments, albeit on a small scale, that do away with the current political system completely. In Bolivia, a small non-profit exists called 'Democracy In Practice', which has experimented with radically new forms of democracy in schools. Rather than holding student elections, they engaged in sortition, a lottery-based system of governance. Students draw lots to see if they are 'elected' onto the student board of government. Electoral terms are shortened, and traditional hierarchical positions (such as president and vice-president) have been abolished.[48] Sortition is of course not new. It was used in ancient Athens to pick magistrates, and it is a process used today to pick jurors for criminal trials. It is arguably one of the more democratic forms of governance, far more so than the parliamentary electoral systems that dominate Western societies. But such experiments, such as those in Bolivian schools, demonstrate that a radical, indeed revolutionary, system of politics is possible, one that shuns parliamentary-style politics completely.

More directly, groups such as UK Uncut are actively using creative and activist forms as resistance to austerity. In 2012, they teamed up with disabled activists to protest outside the headquarters of a company they saw as responsible for a great deal of suffering, namely Atos. With no hint of irony, Atos were one of the sponsors of the 2012 Paralympic Games. The activists used sit-ins, creative media and noisy protests, and highlighted the issues of austerity and the damaging effects the WCA programme was having on people's lives. They utilized creative means of protest: online methods of recruitment beforehand, creative media during (such as music, banners and artworks), and video dissemination after. The protests clearly worked because in 2014, no more than six months after the tragic death of Michael O'Sullivan, Atos had their contract with the government terminated. A small victory, but one that shows how creative forms of resistance can have tangible outcomes.[49]

UK Uncut have also occupied tax-dodging firms' stores and turned them into social service centres, held street parties outside the houses of austerity-implementing politicians, performed public interventions and held one-person protests.[50] They regularly stage occupations, liaise overtly with official groups and operate covertly with more clandestine groups to subvert, resist and creatively appropriate the instigators of austerity to highlight its deleterious and deadly impacts.

These practices (and many, many more besides) highlight how Florida's view of an apolitical creativity that 'drives economic growth' has nothing creative about it other than creating more of the same. Austerity has weaponized this creativity by forcing those not fortunate enough to be in the 1 per cent to live with less. But what UK Uncut and others also show is that there is an alternative ideology of creativity out there, one that actively resists austerity and the broader version of creativity as contributing to capitalism's growth. But because this form of creativity aims to produce worlds in which capitalism cannot take hold, it is castigated by politicians and the mass and social media commentariat as errant, unwanted, undemocratic and damaging. Far from being apolitical, the politics of creativity is crucial.

The political choice before us, then, is that we can be 'creative' in order to maintain the transfer of wealth from the margins to the centre via relentless appropriation, or engage in a radical creativity (such as protest, activism, solidarity networks and so on) that destabilizes those margins so they resist co-option and are allowed to create more just and equitable horizons of possibility. Creativity is, indeed *must* be, political.

4
Technology: Algorithmic Creativity

Just one week before the two aeroplanes flew into the World Trade Center in September 2001, the economic landscape also suffered a momentous shift. It may not have been realized at the time, but there was an event that signalled the turning of the tide of corporate frameworks in the US (and subsequently globally). The shift was from a vertical, hierarchical one-firm structure, to a more horizontal and networked system of multiple companies and firms. This shift symbolically occurred on 3 September 2001, when it was announced that Hewlett-Packard (HP), one of the largest technology companies in Silicon Valley at the time, had bought Compaq, which in turn owned the now defunct Digital Equipment Corporation (DEC).

In the 1980s and 1990s HP and DEC were competitors in the rapidly expanding domestic and commercial markets for personal computers, printers and software. HP were head-quartered in Silicon Valley in California, and DEC were based in the 'rival' tech cluster, Route 128 in Massachusetts. The complex story of their rivalry, and HP's eventual triumph, has played out in academic debates for the past twenty-five years, but it boils down to their vastly different corporate cultures.

HP – and Silicon Valley more broadly – grew during this period by harnessing (or perhaps exploiting) the technological innovations of the rapidly growing community of smaller and more agile software firms around it. Emanating from the mixture of a sun-drenched Californian laissez-faire capitalism and a willingness to take risks with new technologies, the economic culture of Silicon Valley was all about harnessing personal and social networks to power creativity and innovation. AnnaLee Saxenian, an economic geographer and researcher into the history of Silicon Valley, recounts a famous saying by William Hewlett (the co-founder of HP):

> If you want to succeed here [Silicon Valley] you need to be willing to do three things: change jobs often, talk to your competitors, and take risks – even if that means failing.[1]

During the '80s and '90s, Silicon Valley witnessed high rates of company births and deaths, staff swapped jobs regularly (hybridising different companies' ideas), and while firms were highly competitive, they recognized that sometimes they needed to collaborate. Indeed, Saxenian goes on to quote one tech worker who states: 'Many of us woke up in the morning thinking that we were working for Silicon Valley, Inc.'[2]

Ellen Ullman, a tech-worker-turned-novelist, published a book, *Close to the Machine*, in 1997. In it, she charts the development of Silicon Valley and the broader tech industry in the US via this corporate culture of inter-firm linkages, buy-outs and rapid staff turnover. Moreover, she outlines how the tech workers somehow began on a real conscious level to fuse with the code that they were working on, and any semblance of human working capacities, including its ethical considerations, ebbed away. She tells of situations in which 'the machine begins to seem friendlier than the analysts, the users, the managers'.[3] The clarity and pure orderliness of the code became a better world than the messiness of human interactions. It was the coming of age of a corporate culture that mirrored the autonomous complexity of computer code.

On the other side of the country in Route 128 near Boston, HP's rival, DEC, had a far more stringent and hierarchical corporate culture. They didn't integrate with other companies; managers lacked connections to local political and business collectives. Mirroring the more bureaucratic nature of institutional management that pervaded East Coast thinking at the time, DEC was inflexible, and overly determined by management decisions and committee structuring. Preferring bureaucratic knowledge to flair for technological wizardry, DEC shunned the horizontal, freer and more autonomous forms of firm development.

As a result, they were unable to bring their hardware and software products to the market as quickly as HP could. DEC floundered internationally; it began to lose market share, and redundancies were rife. In June 1998 the Japanese technology company Compaq bought DEC, but even that couldn't save it.

So that day, one week before the world shifted its gaze to geopolitical struggles and the new age of Islamist terrorism, HP announced to the world that it had bought Compaq and it instantly became one of the largest and most successful creative technology companies of the 2000s. It turned over upwards of $100 billion in 2006–9, and was ranked ninth in the Fortune 500 in 2009.

Since then, Silicon Valley has eclipsed Route 128 and is now the global epicentre of the creative technology industry. HP's dominance has faded during this time; it has been usurped by firms that have taken the model of agility and autonomy and cranked it up a notch. The new tech behemoths of California – Apple, Facebook and Alphabet (Google's parent company) – have built the culture of the area, drawing on inter-firm networks, social connections, risk-taking business strategies, and personal capacity in order to grow.[4] They have taken the perceived beauty and autonomy of the computer code they were immersed in, and from that, built a global system of economic monopoly.

In essence, it is the mentality of the 'hacker'. Zuckerberg himself was a hacker: that's essentially how he created (or appropriated) the idea for Facebook. But even as a multibillion-dollar corporate leviathan, Facebook still has that individualized culture of hacking. 'Move fast and break things' was Facebook's motto up until 2014 (when

it changed to 'Move fast with stable infra[structure]').
Hacking then became part of the corporate culture of Facebook, and the 'new' Silicon Valley giants. As the journalist
Franklin Foer has written:

> To hack is to be a good worker, a responsible Facebook citizen – a
> microcosm of the way in which the company has taken the language of radical individualism and deployed it in the service of
> conformism.[5]

Engaging in this hacker mentality was not only evident
in how Facebook created new products, but how it grew
as a company. The old form of worker, akin to William
Whyte's 'organization man', was gone: the way to work in
the twenty-first century is to shun management's control
because it denies agility, speed and creativity. Seeking out,
investing in, then taking over young, energetic, bright
and innovative new people and firms mirrored this hacker
ethos. It meant Facebook and the others were able to take
advantage of the flexibility of smaller firms and the regional
culture of creative autonomy to grow.

This is now the standard, high-growth business model,
with tech giants keen to take risks on small scale but promising creative entrepreneurs. The emphasis is on inter-firm
collaboration, project-based work, risk-taking and a 'horizontalization' of creative industrial activity. Also, Silicon
Valley is a magnet for international talent, with people
(often fresh out of colleges of universities from all over the
world) flooding into the area, armed with what they believe

is the next big tech idea, creating a diverse multicultural community.

The stories of the maverick innovator and lone creative 'original' thinker (which, as Chapter 3 outlined, is highly problematic) are intoxicating, and the potential for that big payday when Alphabet or Facebook buys out your small start-up is too great for many to pass up. Hence, Silicon Valley is a creative cluster *par excellence*. It is the model that the world is desperate to emulate.[6]

'Horizontalization' more broadly is a key concept of neoliberal thought. According to Hayek, the godfather of neoliberalism, all phenomena, be it society, markets, humans and even morality, can be explained, and indeed better articulated and realized, by autonomous, decentralized systems. Thinking independently, the ability to be truly self-interested, and intense competition between those individuals, are the fundamental prerequisites for a more progressive society.[7] Hayek's ideas, implemented by the UK and US governments from the '70s onwards, forged an economic landscape that foregrounded the corporate structures that Silicon Valley actively encouraged. It was a landscape that embraced corporate autonomy and economic complexity.

Hayek famously stated that 'competition is a discovery procedure', in which the only way to truly discover new things is to make sure that we do not know the constituency of that competition.[8] In this view, competitive markets are the true 'creative' force of the world because they are 'natural' (that is, they mirror the Darwinian mechanics of evolution and natural selection) and produce new modes of consumption, free from a centralized or overarching controlling and planning force. And if these markets and their internal interactions can be as horizontal, frictionless, decentred, heterogeneous and networked as possible, then consumption patterns will be optimized. The uncomplicated comparison between capitalistic markets and the Darwinian natural world has been, and continues to be, a tenet of neo-liberal thought.[9] This thinking pervades how creativity is thought of in relation to technology; the more technology individualizes us and creates a social world geared toward the monetization of everything, the more money there is to be made. Any social utility of this creative technology is snuffed out in favour of how it can be implemented to feed capitalism's growth.

With the onset of internet technologies in the '90s, smartphones in the 2000s, the proliferations of apps in the 2010s – and the 3D-printed internet of things set to become increasingly the norm in the 2020s[10] – Silicon Valley is embracing a future in which autonomous networked digital information technology will become 'the dominant mode through which we experience the everyday'.[11] The manufacture of digital products has become the most profitable form of industrial production today. More and more smart devices, apps and personal technologies are being produced that penetrate deeper and deeper into our everyday lives, cocooning us from a broader social world, and ensnaring us into another world made up of ones and zeros.

Algorithmic Creativity

Every interaction we have with these technological interfaces produces yet another set of data. As we move around the city, swipe in and out of the subway, order food, message a friend, take a photo of our dinner, order shopping for our smart fridge, swipe right for a late night rendezvous – all these actions are encoded by the technologies that facilitate them. Ones and zeros stream from our daily routine onto the servers of tech companies all over the world. The exabytes of data produced hourly become treasure troves for those wanting to know more about how to commercialize our everyday lives.

This 'big data' is unmanageable, and indeed, unfathomable by human eyes and minds. Hence, software has been developed to scour this information and design ever more creative ways of using it to get us to engage in producing more of the same kind of data. The onset of big data has led some commentators to proclaim that 'data is the new oil' but this new oil has to be drilled for and extracted.[12] And this is where algorithms come in.

An algorithm is simply a set of rules that dictate particular behaviours. One of nature's most magnificent sights, the murmuration of flocking starlings, occurs because of the algorithmic behaviour of each individual bird. Every starling will fly as close as they can to the wing of the next, copying any movement to maintain proximity. But tiny deviations in one bird's movement ripple through the flock, creating the mesmeric swirling and contortion of the mass of starlings.

Within the realm of technology, an algorithm is simply a piece of computational code. It is a programmed instruction (or set of instructions) that dictates an action. There are algorithms embedded with the source code of our web browsers that scour the videos we watch online, and suggest other videos that we might also want to watch. There are algorithms that dictate how we can better bypass traffic on our satellite navigation apps. There are even algorithms that can dictate what food you should eat in the evenings based on your daily activities.

This type of programming brings with it a huge potential for societal progress, development and justice. Take, for example, one of the biggest killers in the world, cardiac arrest (more than 300,000 people die from cardiac arrests in the US every year). Most people will view them as sudden, unexpected events, but the body gives off very subtle clues before they occur. Predicting them has been extremely difficult for human doctors, but a team from Chicago have developed an algorithm that tracks the minute changes of twenty-eight variables (including previous admission patterns, food consumption and so on) and predicts which patients are more likely to suffer an arrest and crucially, when that might be.[13] Similar artificially intelligent software has been developed in Oxford in the UK, which is performing far better than human consultants in picking up the signals of heart attacks and predicting lung cancer. Beyond healthcare, algorithms are used to create driverless cars and real time animation; they are even deployed in the hope that they may predict earthquakes.[14] In addition, there are algorithms that can react, adapt and learn from the massive data sets produced daily. These 'machine learning' algorithms have further layers of code that allow for more complexity, creating autonomous programs that can 'learn' in real time, far quicker than humans ever could.

Algorithms are also becoming creative, mirroring human ingenuity and artistic patterns. In the summer of 2017, Google's 'DeepMind' artificial intelligence team created a virtual robot that taught itself to walk in a basic virtual environment. They gave the robot in the programme relatively simple parameters: sensors to detect the obstacles around it, and information of its orientation. They then created an incentive for it to get from one point of the virtual world to another. But there was no programming for the robot at all about how to move. The results are strikingly similar to how humans walk. It jumps over walls that are low enough, moves around them if they are too high. It is even able to jump over gaps.[15]

This is an example of machine learning: an algorithmic capability in which complex computer codes harvest data and produce learned behaviours and activities that respond entirely on their own. What's more, this machine leaning is able to ape human artistic creativity. In 2016, a team of computer scientists created an algorithm that data-mined the 350 or so existing Rembrandt paintings. Based on all the variations of previous paintings (from *The Night Watch* to *Bathsheba*), the computer code 3D printed what it believed to be a 'typical' Rembrandt, but one that was completely new. It was indistinguishable from a real Rembrandt to all but the most expert of connoisseurs, and the team behind the painting are asking what is next for these algorithms able to produce works of art.[16]

In another show of the impressive creativity of machine learning algorithms, in 2015, the advertising company M&C Saatchi installed a 'smart billboard' at a bus stop in London. 'It's got a genetic algorithm behind it,' said the company, 'and what it's doing is evolving to show the most effective possible ad that it can.'[17] The cameras in the billboard measure how long people look at an advert, and whether they display happy or sad facial characteristics. It then tweaks the adverts with the vast databank of images, texts and layouts available to it. Based on the feedback of viewers, it 'evolves' to create what it believes to be the most eye-catching advert. In essence, it is doing the work of a traditional advertising creative.

If this kind of machine learning is an indication of how artificial intelligence is progressing, we are seeing the embryos of more than just artificial intelligence: we are seeing the birth of an artificial *creativity*. The potential of such a creative technology is indeed limitless. With the power of ever more sophisticated forms of computational and artificial creativity, some of the world's most pressing issues could be tackled head on.

But as of today, the main usages of this technology are to create paintings to sell, and to finesse advertising. Capitalism's ethos of consumption-at-all-costs means that these new creative technologies are being tested and implemented in the service of its enlargement. Far from expanding the horizons of creative possibilities of human endeavour and a more socially just and/or environmentally sustainable world, the technology is closing them down by hawking us more sophisticated advertisements, in the hope that we spend more.

Let's look briefly at one of the most powerful of the tech giants, Google. The company provides 80 per cent of all internet searches globally, and its web browser Chrome has a 50 per cent usage share. But more than its saturation of how we access information, the way in which that information gets delivered is carefully tailored by machine-learning algorithms.

Our personal information, previous searches, browsing habits, how long we spend on each search page, the time of day; these (and countless other variables) are all fed into Google's gargantuan data centres that dominate the rural landscapes around the American South, northern Europe, Chile, Singapore and Taiwan. Once that information is combed by the complex and highly-tuned algorithmic software, we are presented with a set of results subtly tweaked to what they think we as individuals want to see. Crucially, the results at the 'top' of the search are those that get the most traffic, and hence, this is some of the most important digital 'real estate' in the world.

Along with these results, there are the adverts for consumer goods and services that have been summoned by another set of algorithms. These have been curated by Google AdWords, an arm of the company that has succeeded in monetizing every word in every language.[18]

In perhaps Google's most marketized form of computational commercialism, AdWords gives any company with a web presence (which these days is all of them) the chance to 'bid' for words linked to their business. For example, if you run a dog sitting service, when you log in to Google's AdWords, you can select words or phrases that the algorithms suggest for you (presumably words like dogs, pets, lazy dog owner, dog leads etc.), and then bid an amount of money that, crucially, is suggested by algorithms. The ultimate prize that you are bidding for is that your site's URL gets pushed higher up the page ranking, so they appear at the top of the search pages for those phrases you selected. Then, if your link gets clicked on, you pay Google the amount you bid for it.

Therefore, every word has its price to Google; it is an online auction hall for words as pure monetized exchange.[19] And the computation of the prices is increasingly out of the hands of humans as they are derived from complex machine learning, or what Google has described as the 'unreasonable effectiveness of data'.[20]

The law professor Timothy Wu has argued that Google's AdWords has perfected the transformation of our attention and desire for information into an advertizer's dream. He argues that Google are the latest company in a long line of 'attention merchants' that attempt to monetize our attention, wherever it is:

> Google had, in fact, laid bare what had originally been so miraculous about the attention merchant model – getting something truly desirable at no apparent cost.'[21]

Using ever more sophisticated and artificially creative algorithms, Google has created an almost frictionless and thus perfect marketplace, in which the actual meanings of words, and their inherent complexity, is irrelevant. As a result, our attention is being harvested for ever more consumption.

So while machine learning algorithms are potentially world changing, the only thing many of them are changing is the profit margins of Silicon Valley's corporate titans. More specifically, their power to implement these creative algorithms across the globe has extended Hayek-inspired corporate autonomy into the social world. Or, to think about it another way, machine learning extends autonomy and autonomous modes of working deeper into the recesses of the social world. How we access information, form relationships, look for love, find employment, engage in politics, travel, exercise, sleep and even how we breathe are being infested by software and algorithms that are 'learning' from the continually expanding big data we generate every day.

If you layer on top of this the governmental policies and cultural paradigms that praise tech workers as the creative class paragons who will save your city, region or nation from economic stagnation and/or decline, these technology firms have been allowed to spawn multiple copies of themselves across the world.

And then, there is the expanding universe of apps, wearable hardware and online networks focused on the codification and appification of every part of our 24/7 routine.

They atomize our lives into compartments to be measured, ranked, fed into a complex system and ultimately profited from. And they offer no way of escaping them; there is no exit route: you must conform to this way of working or risk alienation from this brave new technological world.

These actions erode any sense of collective sociality and create personal filter bubbles. Google's search functions are specifically tailored for our individual (and individualized) tastes. If we are all presented with subtly different answers, even if we type in the same questions, then this action slowly chips away at a sense of a collectivized body of knowledge. Instead it is replaced by a tailored, atomized individual world view (accompanied by meticulously targeted adverts).

It's not just Google of course. Social media platforms utilize algorithms to curate and individualize content. Who we are connected with, what links we click on, which videos we watch, how we react to specific posts: all this (and more) provides social media algorithms with powerful data to further finesse the streams of information that fly across our screens. If, on Facebook, we click on a link to a particular news article, that provides the algorithm with a little bit more information about what sort of content we are interested in. Whether we clicked on it because of genuine interest, boredom, voyeurism, gratification, or even as an attempt to broaden our algorithmic horizons, the information is completely untethered to the reason it was clicked on. It all goes towards curating, in real time, the feeds we see.

This social media filter bubble that is created, and then continuously curated, limits the range of information we consume and results in the confirmation of political, ethical and moral biases. These platforms 'suggest' who to follow, people to connect with and sites to visit. Because you follow person X who has a posting history, personal profile and online behaviour schematic that is 99.9 per cent similar to person Y, we are offered the chance to follow them as well. The more we click on the links, followers and friends that these algorithms suggest for us, the more specific our feeds become.

This continual finessing of suggestive consumption patterns has even extended into protest movements. When we sign an online petition, for example, we may then be given the message: 'You signed a petition about animal rights; would be interested in signing one about deforestation as well?' Activism, it seems rather ironically, is following the same trajectories as digitized consumption.

Machine learning algorithms hence forge a path for us through the amorphous soup of virtual information, all the while narrowing our field of vision. We have become mere conduits of the flow of capital; our sole purpose is to keep on clicking, to further monetize and hence eradicate the deep, tacit information that language holds.[22] The manipulation of our political, economic, consumptive, ethical and moral behaviour for capital gain is a form of 'algocracy', a governance structure that is based on these machine learning algorithms, and crucially, these are used to replace human-based decision-making.[23]

Those looking to assuage these concerns will point to how much of this artificial creativity is confined to the virtual world. After all, screens can be turned off. However, with the introduction of 3D printing into the mainstream, artificial creativity has within its reach a 'means of production'. In the same way that the Rembrandt painting created by a creative algorithm was 3D printed, the technology exists to allow this artificial creativity to produce material artefacts that cannot so easily be ignored. Artificial creativity has the means to enter the material world.

But, rather than being a dystopian nightmare, 3D printing, or digital fabrication, *can* radically disrupt current capitalist models of production. As Adam Greenfield, author of *Radical Technologies*, has noted:

> Given digital fabrication at scale, the fundamental set of stimuli that underlie all economic behavior would be altered quite out of recognition. A command economy seeks to plan ahead of time what things will be needed, and how many of each will be required; a market economy uses prices as signals to determine what should be made and when. An economy based on personal fabrication would undermine the assumptions common to both, by allowing end consumers to fulfil emergent demand more or less directly.[24]

The social applications of such technology are full of potential to promote social justice. For example the ability to near-instantly produce material infrastructure in those parts of the world that desperately need it radically alters the core-periphery model of global exploitation. The large swaths of urban space currently devoted to storing and stocking the material 'things' we need could be freed up for more pressing social needs (for example, housing).

But as Greenfield also notes, there are powerful forces of traditional capitalism inhibiting the more egalitarian uses of 3D printing. Intellectual property, patent rights and simply the cost of the raw material means that this highly creative and productive technology remains subject to the laws of capitalist production. Indeed, Greenfield argues that 'if we believe that putting this capability into as many hands as possible is a public good worth seeking, then preventing it from being enclosed, packaged and sold as a market commodity is vital'.[25] In other words, 3D printing, along with the machine learning algorithms that may power it, *needs* to shun privatization and embrace more democratic forms of governance if it is to break capitalism's current hold on its creative power.

In sum, the creative industry of Silicon Valley (and its suitors across the world) is commanding and controlling the very material, personal and psychological fabric of our (increasingly less) collective society and its means of production. Its desire to individualize our behaviour and turn away from collective sociality renders us more amenable to complex modes of organisation, and therefore make us easier to profit from. Machine learning algorithms are being developed almost exclusively along the existing contours of societal progress — namely expansion of capitalism. They are almost impenetrable to forms of public or democratic control, the kind of control needed in order to realize their more socially just ends. As such, they are creating nothing but more of the same.

The Sharing Economy

The 'ride hailing' app Uber has had a stratospheric rise to global popularity. The first proper ride was in 2011, and now it is the world's largest taxi company, having made US$6.5 billion in 2016.[26] But, this is on the back of acutely exploitative working practices.

Uber have always maintained that their drivers are self-employed and simply using the company's online architecture to facilitate their own microbusiness. Despite this lexical chicanery, the drivers *are* employees in every other sense; the company pays them directly, they conform to (albeit very loose) codes of conduct, and sign a formal contract. Yet Uber do not offer sick pay, maternity leave, holiday entitlement, a minimum wage and any of the in-work welfare required for humane and just workers' rights. And of course, they end up paying less tax because of this.

Given the 'innovative' nature of this business model, the institutional inertia of employment regulation has failed to keep up with these exploitative new employment frameworks, allowing Uber to profit from unprotected working arrangements.

However, in response to what they saw as Transport for London's (TfL) lax application of regulations on Uber, 'regular' black cab taxi drivers staged a number of protests in London in 2016 and 2017. The trade union that represented black cab drivers argued that such a laissez-faire application of important regulations threatened the safety of passengers.[27] In October 2016, a UK employment court ruled that the company should indeed comply (other countries are following suit). A series of other scandals predicated upon an institutionalized sexist corporate culture and questionable political ties ensnared the company over 2016, culminating in the resignation of their CEO, Travis Kalanick, in June 2017. To further complicate matters for this young company, in September 2017, TfL did not renew Uber's licence, citing 'public safety concerns' (many of the drivers did not undergo the criminal record checks required by TfL).

The subsequent uproar by the 3.5 million Londoners who used Uber was matched only by the smugness of the black cab unions. Uber have appealed, so they can continue to operate, but TfL's ruling is (perhaps) the first indication that the unfettered spread of this precarious labour model is butting up against the public need for regulatory frameworks to protect workers and consumers.

That the so-called 'sharing economy' is on the rise is in part due to the rhetoric that surrounded the growth of the Silicon Valley–moulded creative economy in the early years of the twenty-first century, containing as it did an incessant platitude that the economy was now 'weightless'. Gone was the stuff of industrialized production rolling off the end of factory lines, and tangible goods that you had to physically purchase from an actual store. From production to consumption, software replaced physical tools, online purchases replaced stores, digital content replaced physical things, and digital credit replaced cash.

In this virtual soup of data, knowledge and information that swirled around the world, anybody with an internet connection could access this new world economic order. However, scholarship was, and still is, at pains to emphasize the *materiality* of this virtual economy. [28] The super-cooled servers in hyper-secure mega-bunkers, broadband cables dug into the pavements beneath our feet, the pan-oceanic pipelines, the geostationary satellites above the Earth tracking our every move, the polycarbonate slabs that we have in arms' reach every second of our waking hours: the way digital capitalism works on an inter-personal and daily basis is predicated upon a vast and growing *material* infrastructure – one that is ravenous for resources.

Hence, the creative and digital economies also target the material parts of our lives. The digitization of the economy and its invasion into the minutiae of everyday life has given capitalism impetus to engineer new ways of amassing further profit-generating matter.

So now, there is a myriad of platforms designed to monetize our assets. The business-model *du jour* is to create a digital architecture in which consumers ('users') sign up their 'spare asset' (be that their house, car, spare seat on their short-haul private flight, workspace, wedding dresses or even their job) and lease it out to someone else. The only thing the company provides is the technology and virtual assistance required so that people can 'share' their assets with each other – at a cost.

This sharing economy has been heralded by those who eulogize the power of creativity as a means by which ordinary citizens will replace the corporation as the centres of capitalistic workings.[29] Business gurus and tech company consultants have argued that as people shun large corporations, and turn to peer-to-peer sharing (of course, at a cost), we are witnessing the 'most significant shift in society since the Industrial Revolution'.[30] If someone leases their car to a weekend visitor to the city, the owner gets a tidy sum for not doing much other than handing over a set of keys. Meanwhile the visitor gets a car cheaper than they would if they went to a multinational car hire company, and the icing on the cake is that CO_2 emissions are reduced. It's the proverbial 'win-win' situation.[31]

However, this depends on how one defines 'win'. Some of the first companies to take part in this 'sharing economy' are some of the largest companies on the planet. Others have experienced backlashes against their 'creative' employment structures.

Deliveroo, for example, is careful to refer to their riders as 'independent suppliers' and, like Uber, are facing legal action against their lack of in-work benefits.[32] They are also facing protests from these 'independent suppliers' because of a change in the fee structure. Rather than pay an hourly wage, in early 2017, Deliveroo changed the terms of the contract (in some cases, with just forty-eight hours' notice) to pay per delivery. Citing the usual 'creativity' platitudes of agility and flexibility, Deliveroo argued that this new model made the deliverer act more efficiently – those who could negotiate traffic better, ride faster and work longer hours would receive more money. Despite this, some drivers argued they saw their real per hour wages drop to as little as £1.71.[33]

Clearly corporate scandal is not new and unique to sharing economy firms. But there is an underlying theme that connects these 'new' corporate structures with the exacerbation of the age-old problems of worker and consumer exploitation resulting from 'innovative' and 'creative' corporate practices. Protesting against these platforms is often countered with accusations of Luddism and a fear of progress and the inevitable changing nature of contemporary economic practices. But this mindset is devoid of the value of welfare, protection and the social imperative of work. Accusing protestors of denying progress is a smokescreen for the deliberate attempts to individualize work, and stunt collective action.

The rapid growth of these companies, predicated upon the highly exploitative nature of their working arrangements, lack of workers' rights, unregulated checks and hidden costs is anything but 'creative'. The technological platforms they utilize to smooth access for people needing a ride from a willing driver may be 'new', but it is hardly creative. It is the digital replication of the fundamental requirement of capital accumulation: namely the frictionless connection between producer and consumer.

Moreover, it 'works' through the financial reification of personal belongings, or to use the sharing economy vernacular, 'underutilized assets'. The rhetoric extols the novel creativity of being able to lease your car, in lieu of it lying idle, using a digital platform that allows you to advertise beyond your immediate network. And, crucially, to do it for a profit. The sharing economy, and the hype surrounding the capability of technology to monetize anything that isn't being used 'fully', ignores the very fact that these digital architectures appropriate our belongings for their profit margins.

Indeed, Airbnb doesn't own any rooms or real estate, Uber does not have any cars on its books, and eBay doesn't have any warehouses full of goods. These companies have built their 'success' on online architectures. They are, in fact, making money out of thin air. It has, though, liberated assets that would otherwise be lying dormant and not realising their full use-value.

This is a viable way out of poverty for many. However, the digitization of services is a form of privatization, financialization and individualization of production and consumption that is, as we've seen, symptomatic of the neoliberal paradigm of creativity. These digital platforms, while proclaiming an emancipatory potential for wealth creation, deny the auxiliary processes of social interaction and public engagement, indeed any practice that doesn't lead to further consumption. It shuts down the sociality of the economy. In other words, it negates the very public and social exchange mechanisms that make 'an economy' more than simply a series of interconnected financial transactions.

The sociologist Pierre Bourdieu argued that economic practices are abstracted from social life, and the greater the degree of abstraction, the more damaging to social life that economic realm becomes. The construction of *Homo oeco-nomicus* denies the social embeddedness of *all* economic practices; to model an asocial, apolitical and acultural economy is a recipe for harm.

The sharing economy ratchets up this abstraction. It drives a wedge between social capital and financial reward by encouraging us to view our socialized material networks as reservoirs of potential profit. We begin to view all our collected stuff with green-tinted glasses. Rather than passing it on, how much would that old child's toy fetch on eBay? Could we sublet our apartment while we go travelling for a month rather than letting a homeless friend couch surf? I don't have time to go shopping in charity stores: is there an app that helps me get married in a used wedding dress? Could I monetize the fact that I often make too much bread in the morning for my family by creating an app for bread-sharing that will allow me to sell any leftover bread to people in my neighbourhood rather than deliver it to a food bank? The sharing economy has made making money from our 'stuff' easier than using it for more socialized ends.

In short, the sharing economy has proliferated a universe of apps and digital platforms that have financialized even the most mundane aspects of our daily lives and, as a result, made more invisible any alternative social utility that our unused assets may have. It has appropriated the act of communal and reciprocal giving; it has, as the name bluntly suggests, economized sharing.

Marcel Mauss's seminal work *The Gift* shows how the very acts of giving and receiving are a social glue: deliberately non-financialized 'transactions' designed to engineer the characteristics of social bonds.[34] He empirically articulates the 'potlatches' that exist in Native American, Polynesian and other tribal societies, namely the *totalized* sociality of gift giving. He explores how, in these societies, gifts are given and then reciprocated, and how if there is an 'imbalance' in the perceived value of these gifts, then further reciprocity is shown. In a constant cycle of gift giving and receiving, the broader moral, spiritual and cultural characteristics of the members of that society ebb and flow accordingly, constantly mapping the obligations of each member of society. The result is a community of mutualism in which production of culture, morality, spirituality and a functioning society emanates from the reciprocal exchange of gifts.

Mauss's work has been influential in broader critical sociological studies, exemplifying how pre-capitalist human civilization was built on the non-financialized 'sharing' of resources. With the popularization of the sharing economy and its intense monetization of the objects around us, the act of gift giving as a means to foster social bonds is reduced, and the expectation (or at least the theoretical potential) of a purely financialized transaction is increased.

The sharing economy is dependent on people willing to give up their resources. As such it has accelerated the reduction in purely socialized forms of giving and hence aids in their appropriation by capitalism. In sum, it encourages us to conform to this mantra: if a small profit could be made lending our unused assets to someone with an efficient, idiot-proof digital system, why bother giving it away for free?

To completely undermine the utility of the sharing economy, though, would be naïve. Realizing the 'untapped' reservoir of wealth embedded in the stuff around us reduces the cost of everyday items; it can reduce the need to rely on planet-destroying corporations; it can reduce the hugely problematic (not to mention environmentally damaging) throwaway culture; it provides a means of flexible working (if you're lucky enough to be able to engage in that type of work without the need for in-work welfare). But in economizing sharing, these innovative digital platforms are destroying non-economized and unfinancialized means of social connection.

The sharing of resources free from the expectation of financial reward strengthens the ties that bind. It allows for relationships to be created that would otherwise be curtailed by monetized exchange. Sharing without the express condition of financial reward is a fundamental humane act that undergirds solidarity in the face of external oppression. The sharing of resources strengthens communities, brings together people in need and can have beneficial impacts on the environment (if performed on a large enough scale). But by appropriating and financializing the act of sharing, solidarity and the collective realization of mutual social exchange, sharing economy agents are denying the fuel for societal change beyond capitalism's exploitative mechanisms. By enacting the creativity rhetoric, they are actually destroying the very social fabric that will aid in realizing a creative future beyond the deleteriousness of capitalism.

Agonistic Creativity

By giving us all the hardware and software to operate as individually as possible, and to instantly monetize our possessions and our labour, Silicon Valley has ensured that the emergence of these new creative possibilities is yoked to a capitalist doctrine. Their implementation, thus far, has been largely experimental, but the companies are ignoring some of the fundamental questions about their impact upon the social world, and indeed our own humanity.

For example, in 2016, Microsoft introduced 'Tay', a Tweetbot that responded to users' queries. It was an attempt to create an artificial intelligence that replicated the conversational, perhaps a little jokey style of Twitter's more mainstream users. However, after only sixteen hours, it had to be taken down when it started tweeting racism, Holocaust-denial, calls for genocide and many other extreme views. It was reacting to the tweets it received, but there were no human checks on the output. It was designed to learn as it evolved but very quickly, given the input, evolved into a racist diatribe that mirrored the murkier, troll-laden, bot-infested realms of Twitter.

Algorithms also exist that supposedly predict which people are more predisposed to commit violent crime: for example the Chicago police force's 'heat list', a database compiled by an algorithm that scours crime data and personal records. Critics have argued that the algorithms used, as well as being opaque (the Chicago police are currently being sued to release the code), are replicating racial bias. The result is that many young black men are being targeted as potential violent criminals because of simply where they live, or who they know.[35]

The computer scientist Zeynep Tufekci has long argued that while machine learning has all the inherent biases of the 'real world', this is ignored because it is seen as computational and objective. She gives the example of the summer of 2014, in which both the Ferguson riots and the Ice Bucket Challenge reached their zenith. Facebook's news feed algorithms are 'optimized for interaction', so those posts that are more liked, shared, commented on and viewed will be moved higher up the feed. Reacting to the Ferguson riots doesn't conform to such behaviour as much as the Ice Bucket Challenge does (it's more morally comfortable to 'like' a video of your friend having ice thrown all over them than it is a picture of institutional racism at its most violent). As such, the algorithms skewed news feeds to downplay the riots, effectively hiding them from view.[36]

The issue with many of these machine learning algorithms, and the rush to experiment with them (particularly those predicated upon the input of 'big data' and that are programmed to learn in relation to that data), is that they operate free from human input; they are computational black boxes. As such, they are following Hayek's mantra of the discovery procedure as progress, making sure that the constituency of systems is unknown so as to ensure ultimate 'fairness' (or objectivity) of competition. But in some of the more insidious applications of such algorithms, this 'unknown' quality is being used predictively.

Who is most likely to commit violent crime in Chicago is one thing, but there are also algorithms that are designed to find out which candidate would be best for a job, or which child will grow up to be a terrorist.[37] Many of these algorithms have been created and applied for commercial, political and militaristic reasons. They have millions upon millions of lines of code, each one adapting to the granular data it mines off the myriad of digital crumbs we leave behind. All the while they are replicating the biases of these crumbs, soaking up very human prejudices and replicating them under the guise of faux-neutrality.

In this algocracy, it is even more critical to hold on to the creative processes of human sociality – a sociality that does not conform to the ideologies of pure autonomy and ever-more complexity. Tufekci goes on to argue that the response should be to strengthen our resolve to make sure human morality and ethics are not part of these algorithms' decision-making processes. In other words, 'We cannot outsource our moral responsibility to machines.'[38] Many algorithms have been created to aid in the process of human creativity and discovery. They can help predict cardiac arrests and lung cancer, make healthcare provision more efficient, and get us to where we need to be quicker. Yet, as we have seen, they absorb unjust biases and reflect them back to us as if that were the natural state of things. They can amplify existing racial, sexist, ageist and ableist tendencies that, as Chapter 3 showed, are inherent in capitalism's power structures.

To counter these injustices we require a collaborative effort. Here we can turn to the political theorist Chantal Mouffe, who has argued that confrontation between opposing views forms the basis of a democratic process, one that seeks alternative horizons beyond the prevailing mode of capitalist production. This is a form of *agonistic* politics, one in which dissensus is key. She argues:

> In the pluralist democracy, disagreements about how to interpret the shared ethico-political principles are not only legitimate but necessary. They allow for different forms of citizenship identification and are the stuff of democratic politics. When the agonistic dynamics of pluralism are hindered because of a lack of democratic forms, then passions cannot be given a democratic outlet. The *ground is therefore laid* for various forms of politics articulated around essentialist identities of a nationalist, religious or ethnic type, and for the multiplication of confrontations over non-negotiable moral values, with all the manifestations of violence that such confrontations entail.[39]

Being creative is thinking of entirely new ways of organizing society, ways that seek to collectivize rather than individualize. As Mouffe argues, such thinking cannot happen without dissensus. Indeed without it, the 'ground is laid' for the already existing unjust hegemonic systems to fight over which should be in control. To break that cycle, to enter the *unstable* ground that a radical creativity affords, this dissensus is critical.

Yet those algorithms that reaffirm our world view – those that curate the daily information, content or political opinion that form a frictionless experience of the world – actively avoid this agonism. Social media filter bubbles close out alternative worldviews. Having individualized information spoon-fed to us by search engines negates frustrating encounters with opposing and counterfactual information. Being able to sell our unused possessions to a faceless customer online stops us from thinking about who might benefit from having it given to them for free. Neatly curating our friendship circles online stops us from encountering strangers in the virtual commons.

Compounding the damaging effect of these filter bubbles, there are very few 'ways out' of this world. Social media is crowding out offline media (and is, rather ironically, becoming far less social). Ways of information-gathering that aren't online searches are dying out. Sharing economy apps are not directing us to think twice before monetizing our assets. Society looks with increasing suspicion upon people who go 'offline' to generate relationships. In order to assuage the damaging effects of this technological and machine-leaning creativity and maintain an agonistic society, we need to start creating digital platforms with exit routes in-built – we need to be able to unplug as easily as we can plug in.

Furthermore, the atomistic thinking and the curating of the self that algorithms effortlessly reproduce are the antithesis of the sociality and agonistic encounters that a radical creativity requires. Algorithms and the sharing economy have allowed for hyper-individualism and a lazy acceptance that machine intelligence is a neutral force in the world. They have smoothed out the erratic, agonistic and unpredictable nature of everyday sociality between chronically imperfect human beings, and imposed programmatic behaviour that can be harvested for investment opportunities to sell back to us in the future. These digital products map out our horizon, futures that consist of nothing more than a financialized intensification of the present mode of capitalist consumption.

To break this cycle is to collectively destabilize that future, render it infertile to the outputs of Silicon Valley, and reaffirm the agonistic social bonds that make us very *un*algorithmic: that which makes us human. To quote the art critic and writer Jonathan Crary:

> Experiences now consist of sudden and frequent shifts from absorption in a cocoon of control and personalization, into the contingency of a shared world, intrinsically resistant to control. The experience of these shifts inevitably enhances one's attraction to the former, and magnifies the mirage of one's own privileged exemption from the apparent shoddiness and insufficiency of a world in common. Within 24/7 capitalism, a sociality outside of individual self-interest becomes inexorably depleted, and the interhuman basis of public space is made irrelevant to one's fantasmatic digital insularity.[40]

5
The City: Concrete Creativity

In July 2017, the London mayor, Sadiq Khan, launched the first 'London Borough of Culture' competition. In a fanfare of glossy advertising videos and promotional material, Khan offered £1 million of arts funding to any London borough that could put together a programme of events that 'celebrates its creativity'. The video that accompanied the launch includes a montage of cultural activities performed by ethnically diverse people. From graffiti artists to classical musicians, the video is a celebratory offering of the vast array of creative and cultural activities that are present in London.

The text of Khan's narration of the video is as follows:

London is the cultural capital of the world. Our communities and neighbourhoods are a rich tapestry of creativity and originality, which illustrate the diversity of expression that makes London such a vibrant city. And right now, culture in the capital is more exciting than ever. That's why, as mayor of this great city, I'm proud to be launching the first ever London Borough of Culture Competition. Each London borough has the opportunity to win the chance to deliver a cultural programme that brings people and ideas together. Culture has the incredible power to transform lives, build new friendships, tell new stories and write new histories. Now is the time for your borough to step up, to celebrate its creativity, its collaboration and its character. Be awarded the title of London Borough of Culture, and show London just how inspiring your borough can be.[1]

Modelled on the 'European city of culture' and 'UK city of culture' schemes implemented by the EU and the UK respectively, this competition will see the winning boroughs adopting the title of London's Borough of Culture (and the £1 million funding) across 2019 and 2020. As can be read from the narration of the video the competition invites boroughs to 'celebrate their creativity, collaboration and character'. The online application form, among other aspirational, yet conspicuously vague questions, asks them to 'consider how your programme will be amazing, ambitious, authentic and all-embracing'.

Notwithstanding the penchant for assonance, the narrative of this competition highlights how creativity is being mobilized within urban development. Containing the usual platitudes about collaboration, originality, authenticity and so on, this policy vehicle is a microcosm of the broader phenomenon of the 'creative city' and how it is manifesting itself in the sociopolitical landscape.

Overall, it signals how creativity has become a byword for the economization of culture. By forcing boroughs to compete with one another for arts funding that would previously have been part of direct governmental finance, it has implemented what is essentially an austerity programme with a fine veneer of a Saturday night reality TV 'winner-takes-all' format. In short, it symbolizes the esoteric, vacuous, yet highly instrumental rhetoric of the creative city script – one that is now over two decades old.

The Creative City

Wynwood is a small neighbourhood district of Miami, Florida. The area is, or at least was, characterized by small-scale industry, largely auto-repair shops and warehouses, with a large Puerto Rican community.[2] But in 2009, a real estate developer called Tony Goldman led an ambitious project to transform the neighbourhood into an 'outdoor street art gallery'. His company, Goldman Properties (now run by his daughter Jessica after his death in 2012), purchased large swaths of industrial property in the area, and attempted to lure international street artists to come and paint murals on the expansive exterior warehouse walls. In a deliberate attempt to 'curate' an outdoor space and use it to catalyse inward investment, the company, backed by a local government desperate for finance, have acted out the creativity script, line by line, to develop the area. This is what Jessica Goldman has to say about Wynwood:

People want to be a part of something that's creative, and we wanted to create the centre for the creative class. We wanted to create a neighbourhood that was geared toward creative people. We are neighbourhood revitalisers ... In a neighbourhood like where we are today, in Wynwood there's not anything really historic about the neighbourhood but what was here was street art. And it wasn't really curated.[3]

Notwithstanding the disregard for local histories or incumbent community, the use of the vacuous banalities ripped almost directly from Richard Florida's book is telling. It tells of how businesses with a vested interest in profitable real estate are using (and abusing) the creativity script for the purposes of gentrification. It tells of how a once subversive, political and illegal activity such graffiti has been co-opted by an urban capitalist agenda.[4] And finally, it tells of how creativity has been used as a flimsy pseudonym for real estate–led gentrification and 'placemaking' on a large scale.

In response to the urban decline and economic stagnation that Wynwood was experiencing after the 2008 crash, a 'business improvement district' (BID) unit was set up, which changed zoning laws and tax rates in order to attract cultural and creative consumption. Galleries, bars, cafés and the right kind of housing that 'young, smart knowledge-based workers will want' were encouraged.[5] Cultural and 'creative' types were lured by a 'walkable urban environment' that included mixed road use – such as shared space for cars and pedestrians – and upscale-but-not-quite-luxury housing units. This now-common trope of 'new urbanism' design was how the 'human scale' neighbourhood was to be developed.[6] Indeed the chair of the BID argued: 'This is the most comprehensive way of thinking about a neighbourhood.'[7]

What sets this example apart from other creative city policies that litter the world's cities is the Wynwood Walls scheme. It is the 'radical' creative development that sets Wynwood out from the crowd (but not too radical so as to deter inward capital investment, of course). It is the project that will earn it global attention in lifestyle magazines, TV and online news outlets. It is the symbol of hip, bohemian and funky creativity and culture that will attract the creative professional workers, and the millions of dollars they bring with them. Of this, Wynwood's management actors – local government, BID and invested real estate companies – have made no secret.

Indeed, there has been a brazen whitewash of Wynwood's history, community, culture and social issues. As a neighbourhood, it had very little in the way of a local art scene to begin with.[8] It didn't have the rich histories of other inner-city areas, but that is irrelevant; it was still a home and a *place*. But in a deliberate attempt to unmake that place, the neighbourhood was deliberately downplayed in the development narrative, almost to suggest as if nothing existed there before at all.

Jessica Goldman, for example, stated in the promotional material that they bought up the real estate 'because nobody wants it'.[9] Whether the poorer incumbent Latino communities were asked if they wanted it for much-needed affordable housing or other important social services, is unclear. What is clear is that this particular creative city script disregarded any of the place's cultural, social or even economic specificities in favour of the 'new' script of upscaling and 'revitalizing' (read, gentrifying) the neighbourhood to cater for a more affluent, white, creative class.

Wynwood is hence a contemporary iteration of an urban policy that is decades old. Ever since the term 'creative city' was first articulated in policy realms by Charles Landry and Franco Bianchini in the late 1990s, it has been used as a vehicle for the kind of urban redevelopment witnessed in Wynwood, and countless other neighbourhoods and cities all over the world.

The deprivation and economic stagnation that Wynwood experienced post-2008 had occurred in many deindustrializing northern UK cities and the rust belt cities of the US in the '70s and '80s. It was marked by blight, crime, ghettoization, and intense poverty. 'White flight', and suburbanization more broadly, saw inner cities hollowed out, with capital chasing the middle classes out to the fringes. Immigrant and working-class populations were left with chronic disinvestment, systemic neglect and a lack of public funds.

The 'creative city' policy was seen as a means of 'reviving' these deprived urban areas. It was tied up with the 'back to the city' movement that saw young, often childless, degree-educated and more mobile people returning to the inner city areas. They were moving there to take advantage of the cheaper rents, as well as looking to capitalize on the opportunities taking shape in light of the deregulation of the financial markets in the '80s and '90s.[10]

There are multiple 'strands' to creative city development strategies, many of which have become incredibly formulaic in their implementation. Much of the advocacy of the 'creative city' was formulated in rather vague and nebulous notions of 'encouraging creativity'. Making urban space affordable for artists, encouraging participation in cultural events, celebrating multiculturalism and local cultures: many of the 'recommendations' of the creative city project were little more than nods to the broader structural shifts toward the enterprising self, autonomy and privatization of space. More concrete was the uptake of these recommendations by urban managers, who in the 1990s and 2000s began to 'encourage creativity' by implementing policies and development schemes that, while having a 'new' cultural and creative aesthetic veneer, continued to have gentrifying effects.

One of the most notable ways in which this happened was the building of large-scale 'flagship' cultural projects. The Guggenheim in Bilbao, opened in 1997, is a successful (at least economically) example of how parachuting a large, expensive, and culturally-significant institution into a declining area can help revive economic fortunes. The museum turned a dilapidated and underused dock area into a thriving cultural and tourist hot spot. It cost approximately €100m to build, a sum that the council claimed to have made back in increased tourism and tax revenues in the first four years of operation.[11] This opened the floodgates with a raft of other cities attempting to replicate the 'Bilbao effect'. Some were strikingly similar in architecture, implementation and indeed economic effects, such as the Taubman Museum of Art in Roanoke, Virginia. Others were not quite so successful – such as Curve in Leicester, UK, which required hardship funds from central government to stay open. Some never made it to construction, such as the Syrian National Museum in Damascus.[12]

But in all cases, it led to the homogenization of the cityscape and urban policy along the same lines of cultural and creative consumption. Alongside the flagship developments, creative city policies have come to be completely normalized in urban development. Most new urban policy documents include some intense (re)branding of a city's cultural offerings along 'cultural' and 'creative' lines. Nightlife, arts scenes, café cultures and so on are aggressively used in marketing material for cities and neighbourhoods as a means to attract creative class workers.

To make sense of this, one only has to watch the branding video for Lincoln, Nebraska.[13] Made in 2012, the video proclaims:

Exciting things are happening in our city; big things. Our spirit has a renewed sense of energy and there's enthusiasm in our collective voice. You can feel it in the streets; you can see it on the skyline. You can hear it in the ideas of our young entrepreneurs and creative class.

While there is a thriving music scene locally, the city's principal employers are the State of Nebraska and the educational system.[14] The main outputs of Lincoln and the wider region are agricultural: cows and corn.[15] Nebraska was the worst performing US state economically in the first half of 2017, with its output declining by 4 per cent.[16] Demographically, the city is 86 per cent white. In many ways, it is a typical US mid-sized city, dependent upon more traditional industries that are struggling to survive.

The video, though, displays vibrant nightlife, craft-based industries, high-end services, walkable streetscapes, cultural and subcultural activities, and a multicultural social milieu. This is an aesthetic that has become the new baseline level of what a city *should* be. In order for Lincoln to change around its economic fortunes, it has done what countless other cities have done: turned to the creative city playbook and followed the protocols step by step.

Along with branding the city as 'creative', changes to the built environment will have the rhetoric of the creative city buried within them. Cities will 'beautify' public space (as well as making it private and curtailing what kind of behaviour is acceptable) with non-descript public art and outdoor play activities. Sydney's creative city policy of 2014 contained many of these schemes. The Darling Harbour area, for example, was rebranded as a 'cultural ribbon', and they placed a few hammocks, outdoor table tennis tables and a smattering of newly branded way-finders.[17] Other strands include the deliberate imposition of creative industry zoning in the form a cultural or creative quarter. Invoking Jane Jacobs's adage that 'new ideas must use old buildings', the 'creative quarter' that utilizes old industrial units or even constructs them anew is as homogeneous as it is ubiquitous.[18]

Finally, the rise of 'placemaking' as a strategy of urban renewal also has echoes of the creative city policy. In 2010, a white paper produced for the National Endowment for the Arts (NEA) in the US proclaimed that:

> Creative placemaking animates public and private spaces, rejuvenates structures and streetscapes, improves local business viability and public safety, and brings diverse people together to celebrate, inspire, and be inspired.[19]

Placemaking brings together local communities, government, local businesses and public institutions. Its modus operandi is to commission outdoor art projects, community-based infrastructure and pedestrianization schemes; all with the aim of 'foster[ing] entrepreneurs and cultural industries that generate jobs and income'.[20] Spawning initiatives such as Tactical Urbanism, Pop-up City, Urban Acupuncture and others, placemaking is the lexicon by which urban managers and developers leverage community resources and ideas, and implement them as gentrification schemes.[21] Infected with the narrative of austerity (and with more than a whiff of Cameron's 'Big Society' discussed in Chapter 4), placemaking uses the 'creative' energies of local communities to make places more amenable to the influx of the creative class.

Placemaking as a strategy of urban development plays on the urban imaginary of decline; there is no *place* here, so let's make one. It is in the same vein as terms such as 'revitalization' (which was used in Wynwood's case), 'urban renaissance' and 'renewal' that are deliberately invoked to claim a site of gentrification; as if the site being developed were not *vital* already to the people who live, work or play there.

The creative city then exhibits a mixture of many of these strategies. They may or may not reference directly the need to be creative, but much of the new city development agenda will be modelled on the need to attract creative people, and therefore be a precursor to gentrification.

There is another 'strand' to the creative city, though, that is equally damaging. The ubiquity of these cultural and creative urban strategies means that cities lose their distinctiveness. The sterile cultural quarters and beautified places begin to lose their desirability for the creative people a gentrifying city needs. Therefore, creative city protagonists look to create a different place, one that shuns the aesthetics of a large Guggenheim or an overtly beautified and micromanaged streetscape. The 'new' creative city needs to have a veneer of 'edginess', appeal to hipsters and maintain a radical, progressive and perhaps even anti-capitalist aesthetic, all the while mobilizing these (now stabilized) aesthetics for the same traditional purpose: wealth generation for the elite.

Returning to the example of the Wynwood Walls, we see this process in full flow. Street art is now an essential ingredient in fabricating an 'edgy' creative urban neighbour-hood, precisely because it can mobilize these traditionally 'resistive' and anti-capitalist themes in the service of prof-itability. The use of a non-politicized, contemporary art 'scene', coupled with a cosmopolitan night-time economy, completely glosses over social strata that characterize urban neighbourhoods. Moreover, this process glosses over the injustices that come to fore with this type of development: namely the suppression and/or fetishization of marginal and minority groups (race, gender, class and diffability) for profitable gain.[22]

It has been argued that Wynwood's by-the-book creative city development has been 'post-race': it utilizes ethical and racial diversity as tools to promote cosmopolitanism (as per Miami's 'global city' script), rather than to highlight racial and gendered inequalities.[23]

Galleries, public art and hyper-commodified street art play to a particular version of aesthetic consumption that is high-culture and overly white. It is art that is 'aware' of ine-quality within urban space, but 'performs' this as part of a consumption cycle. The knowledge of protest and critique toward such injustices is *given* to an audience to consume rather than as something to enact. Therefore creativity in this rhetorical world is just a pastiche of consumption, more often than not modelled on the consumption patterns of white, middle-class people.

The street artists invited to paint on the warehouses to create the Wynwood Walls came from all over the world (although, it must be said, the promotional videos show virtually no female artists) and the murals contain racial and oriental imagery. But their work is devoid of the subversive sentiments that might highlight and actively work against inner-city racial inequalities.

Part of the corporate appeal of globalized street art is that it contains just enough radical and political symbolism for audiences to feel they have engaged in a resistive act by simply appreciating it. It is part of the broader industrial media production that performs our anti-capitalism for us.[24] But any racial, orientalized or 'othered' imagery within street art (or within the art galleries and public art pieces that surround them in Wynwood or any other creative city replicas from around the world) is absorbed into the broader 'post-race' narrative of cosmopolitanism. The creative city script, that Wynwood (and indeed the imagery around London's Borough of Culture competition) has exemplified so perfectly, celebrates race and ethic diversity, but only as a precursor to gentrifying development. More damagingly, it fails to address the causes of these racial tensions; indeed it benignly exacerbates them.

Artwashing: The Art of Creative Gentrification

As well as mobilizing race and ethnicity to bloat their wealth, creative city protagonists use gender, class and diffability. The geographer Heather McLean, who has researched community arts practices in Toronto, has highlighted how care and social reproductive work are devalued forms of labour within the creative city.[25] In the study, she identified how in parts of Toronto, creative city development agendas incorporated 'feminist-inspired planning models' that included social care work (such as people working with disadvantaged youths); but rather than reproducing environments of sustained care they were directed toward gentrification, specifically as rhetorical vehicles to compete for investment. Having socially responsible activities embedded in the creative city script makes for great PR. In other words, the planners had taken the feminist ethics of the planning models and 'stripped [them] of concerns for economic equality or social justice'.[26]

Much like 'creative work' in general, the creative city script of flagship developments, branded videos and creative quarters leaves little room for an appreciation of the highly gendered nature of social and emotional labour. Focusing on specific feminist community arts practice in Toronto, McLean finds merit in their ability to open up spaces of critique toward overtly white, middle-class, and family-orientated policy.[27] In articulating these critiques, they have tangible results in stemming injustices that flow from the implementation of the creative city.

However, the study also recognizes that much of this artistic work is co-opted to 'groom' neighbourhoods and attract investment. In essence, Toronto's neighbourhoods used the work of feminist community-based art as a means of branding that place as artistically unique and socially engaged, in the hope of attracting inward investment. This is what has been called 'artwashing',[28] and it is here we find another contemporary 'tactic' of creative city development.

Corporate finance has always been used to amass private collections of contemporary art.[29] But recently, oil corporations have begun sponsoring major cultural institutions, such as BP's backing of the Tate since 1990. As well as providing cheap advertising (BP paid £150,000 a year to Tate, enough for a two-minute primetime TV advert), this softens the corporate image of BP, allowing them the social capital to continue plundering the planet's resources in pursuit of more profit.[30]

In 2010, an activist group called Liberate Tate began a campaign of interventions in and around Tate London and Tate Britain. They shed light on the sponsorship deal with provocative installations, interventionist performances and subversive practices. In perhaps one of the most striking, on 20 April 2011, the first anniversary of the Deepwater Horizon oil spill, a man stripped naked in the main hall of Tate Britain, while two veiled figures poured an oil-like substance over him.[31] These antagonistic artistic protests continued and in 2016 BP ended its sponsorship of Tate.

The concealment of ethically dubious corporate activity under an artistic and cultural veil, i.e. artwashing, is not limited to oil companies. It is also a tactic of the institutions, both public and private, responsible for the gentrification causing a chronic housing crisis in many cities all over the world. New York, for example, prides itself on having cleaned up the homelessness and rough sleeping 'problem' in the '80s and '90s (albeit with the help of rather violent zero-tolerance policing methods).[32] Yet today, the lack of affordable homes has caused an acute homelessness problem. The current provision of 661 shelter buildings for homeless people is at maximum capacity, with plans to open 90 more. The problem has been exacerbated by a rapid increase in rental costs, far outstripping rises in income.[33]

There is a similar story in London, where there is a chronic undersupply of genuinely affordable homes. Those labelled 'affordable' by councils are 80 per cent of market rates, and are anything but 'affordable' to the average worker. As a result, homelessness is at record levels, estimated at 170,000 people in 2016.[34] In addition, council housing is being destroyed and tenants displaced across the country.

For example, Cressingham Gardens is a low-rise, medium-sized council housing estate near Brixton in South London. It is next to Brockwell Park, has panoramic views over the city, and is in many respects an idyllic garden city in microcosm. It is a far cry from the tall, brutalist mass-housing blocks so often the stereotyped view of council housing. But Brixton and Lambeth are experiencing an influx of the creative class, which is pushing up property prices: Cressingham Gardens is now prime real estate.

As a result, the vultures of gentrification have been circling. In 2015, Lambeth Council earmarked the estate for 'regeneration', a pseudonym for demolition and replacement with luxury accommodation. The residents (many of whom are life-long council tenants) were told they must move out, having been offered compensation way below market levels for their properties.[35] The rationale from the council for the redevelopment was that refurbishment was too expensive, and hence there was only one viable option that the council forwarded to the residents: a full demolition and redevelopment, financed by a private real estate company.[36]

Large profit margins are needed to entice investment, and such margins only come with the development of the kind of accommodation that the incoming creative class requires. The counter-argument made by residents is, of course, that all this is smoke and mirrors to safeguard the profitability of the project. Councils themselves profit from wealthier residents two-fold: they get a higher tax base, and the fiscal burden of social housing requirements is displaced geographically to another borough. Such a hike in the bank balance at a time when local budgets are getting squeezed tighter by national government is an intoxicating incentive; one that many councils across London are unable to resist.

In the case of Cressingham Gardens, Lambeth Council obfuscated information when it was requested by a residents' activist group. It commissioned questionable surveys that found 'overwhelming' evidence that supported their case for demolition. It banned resistance groups from meeting in council venues, and other nefarious tactics of disavowal.[37] After a long, exhausting and (at the time of writing) still ongoing legal dispute, the fate of Cressingham Gardens is unclear, with the uncertainty, precariousness and domicidal practices of the council taking their toll on the residents, as they continue to resist the 'redevelopment' of the estate.

Such resistance is widespread in London and across many cities experiencing a chronic housing crisis. In order to counter such resistance, new tactics are needed by those who stand to make vast profits from this kind of estate regeneration. Enter artwashing. Similar to the processes used by oil companies, this kind of artwashing, as the researcher and activist Stephen Pritchard has argued, is a process that harnesses localized (and often unwitting) social capital to 'turn the benign into the terrible; interpersonal relationships and dynamics into global statistics and generic standards; people reduced to little contributions to the financial bottom line.'[38] Artwashing, therefore, is the instrumentalization of art as a means to secure future profitable gain.[39]

The classic theory of arts-led gentrification is that dilapidated inner-city areas are colonized by aspiring artists and bohemians looking for new places to gain artistic inspiration from, not unlike the story of Wynwood. As they embed themselves in the area in low-cost rental accommodation, guardianships or even squats, they begin to foster an atmosphere (or to use a tired urban policy trope, 'vibe') that becomes attractive to creative class professionals.[40] Before long, a place is labelled the 'new' Shoreditch, Williamsburg, Kreuzberg, Fitzroy or Mission District. Property developers all want a slice of the rocketing rents; bars, galleries and clubs all want to open there; and magazines want to feature it.

Of course, while this is happening, the local residents and their way of life are being displaced. The usual mechanisms by which local, usually working class, immigrant and ethnic communities get displaced is by rapidly rising rents, but they also see their local services make way for those befitting the new creative class clientele. More recent years have seen perhaps a more callous mechanism of domicide, with the deliberate reappropriation of working-class aesthetics and/or trivialization of violence for monetary gain.

Take, for example, the Job Centre bar in Deptford in East London that opened in 2014. Previously the building had actually been a job centre, in an area consistently in the top ten per cent of UK boroughs for youth unemployment.[41] The bar's owners claim that it is being sensitive to the history of the area, but such rhetoric only highlights how creative city gentrification practices are now hijacking working class sensibilities for pure branding purposes. Unemployed people in the area are now not only down one job centre, they are being mocked by the very businesses that are pricing them out of their neighbourhood.

Similarly, in Crown Heights in Brooklyn, a newly opened café advertised itself on social media with a picture of a cocktail in front of a bullet-hole riddled wall, stating: 'Yes, that bullet hole-ridden wall was originally there and, yes, we're keeping it.'[42] In an area that experiences high crime and murder rates relative to the rest of New York, the establishment has been accused of crass insensitivity and the trivialization of gun crime.

Both of these instances can perhaps be explained away as poorly judged and insensitive branding exercises. But the fact that they were even attempted is symptomatic of an engrained appropriative 'washing' mechanism in creative city development. Taking local sensibilities and using them as a branding motif is a common strategy of property development (such as the Custard Factory in Birmingham, a creative quarter named after the repurposed building's old use, and many, many others all over the world). But when these sensibilities are of joblessness and violent crime, the branding becomes antagonist and harmful.

This is why the term 'artwashing' is now being used within the context of gentrification: any artistic intervention commissioned, paid for and instigated by developers is viewed as a cynical attempt to make an area amenable to the tastes of the creative class. This artwashing process comes in many guises, from commercial street art commissioned by real estate companies to make a place feel more like Shoreditch to a more complex and longer-term attempt to embed artists in council housing blocks to make it a 'trendy' place to be.

The Balfron Tower in east London, completed in 1967 and designed by Ernö Goldfinger, in a brutalist style, is an example of the latter. In 1996, because of its iconic status, notable architect and striking position on the London landscape, it became Grade II listed, meaning it cannot be altered at all without relevant consent (and demolition becomes almost impossible). As a result, in 2007, the owners (the local council of Tower Hamlets) handed it over to Poplar Harca, a housing association. This transfer was completed after a consultation with the residents, in which they were promised a full refurbishment of their flats. This was badly needed as the tower had fallen into disrepair after decades of financial neglect by the council. With that promise, the residents voted overwhelmingly to sell.

Poplar Harca, as a housing association, has done more for the area than the council ever could. However, their management of the Balfron has been decidedly less reasonable. They offered residents alternative (permanent if required) accommodation while the renovations were to be carried out, or the option to stay on and live with the disruption. Some did move out with the promise of a return date, but many others opted to stay.[43] The assumption was that there would always be a portion of the tower that would remain social housing.

By 2017, the 'right to return' had been removed, and the tower block is now empty. All flats are to be sold off privately, or have been already.[44] Accusations that Poplar Harca were deliberately 'decanting' social residents to offer the flats to wealthier creative class–type professionals (who would benefit from the astonishing panoramic views over London and its proximity to Canary Wharf) were not helped by a promotional video that was put online then quickly taken down. The video played on the cultural mythologies of the 'swinging Sixties' and the building's now kitsch brutalist style, and offered a glitzy and playful version of the tower.[45]

As well as this early promotion of flats to the wealthy elite, the role of Poplar Harca has been characterized by persistent obfuscation. Blaming the financial crash; saying that they had been denied planning permission to build alternative accommodation; dwindling funds: they often responded to questions from residents with, 'We just don't know yet.'[46]

How did they get away with this land grab of houses from the urban poor to give to the elite? It wasn't just with rhetorical chicanery: they engaged in aggressive 'artwashing' practices. Poplar Harca formally partnered with arts organisations to provide short-term residencies to artists, as well as staging performances in the tower. In one of the first schemes, in 2010, Simon Terrill was commissioned by Bow Arts (a local artists' organisation) to produce a long-exposure photograph of the building, with the residents invited to participate by posing on their balconies. Accompanying drawings and text was an online collection of images and a nearby exhibition, all of which brought the Balfron's architectural significance into the mainstream media spotlight.[47] It catalysed the appeal of now 'in vogue' brutalist structures across the UK, bringing the much-maligned architectural style back into the popular imaginary.

A few years later, in 2014, a theatre company performed a modern retelling of Macbeth, which fetishized the imposing brutalist style of the block, as well as its state of disrepair. In keeping with the 'immersive theatre' trend, the audience were invited to follow the actors around the block all night, sleep in specially designed and designated flats and have breakfast on the rooftop in the morning. Notwithstanding the innovative use of the architecture to host a quirky reimagination of Shakespeare, the emphasis of the performance was on its desolate and barren settings. Indeed, one of the theatre company's founders said, 'the building is violent and stark on the skyline', and reviews said that it took place in a 'decaying' tower block. [48] The performance itself, as well as the commentary in the media, ossified the Balfron's image as a decaying, derelict and desolate structure. The fact that, in order to navigate through the building, some of the actors had to squeeze past actual residents would intimate that the building was not as derelict as they suggested.

Other projects included a 'carnival of events' in June 2014 sponsored by the British Council. There were dance groups, beat boxers, artistic exhibitions in empty flats, and artistic tours by commissioned artists. These one-off artistic and creative events cemented the Balfron in the public imagination, giving it an aura of cool and mystique, showcasing it as an edgy but quirky place to live, or at least invest in. As well as these celebratory events, artists were given use of the empty properties with the promise of support, but it soon became clear they were being used to give the building a veneer of artistic credence, a vanguard of 'cool' to help sell the building to the city's creative industry 'thought-leaders' and trendsetters.

This story is particularly acute for Rab Harling, a freelance artist who moved into the tower under the scheme run by Bow Arts. After being offered a flat for a relatively cheap rent, he began a process of visually documenting the lives of the tower's residents. [49] However, he soon found that Bow Arts were actively hostile to him and many of the other artists they were renting the flats to. Rogue inspections, withholding of important residential information: Rab has documented in detail how he believes this was all part of the artwashing and decanting process. [50] But when he called them out on it, they evicted him. Another freelance artist was commissioned by Poplar Harca to do a 'storytelling project' with the residents, which she subsequently posted online. While the project allowed residents to air their concerns about the redevelopment and provided a platform for anti-gentrification stories to be told, she was alerted to the problems of artwashing by Rab on Twitter, and subsequently mused herself whether or not she was complicit in the artwashing agenda.[51]

The fact that it is artists themselves speaking out against artwashing, as well as local residents (often, they are both), adds a layer of complexity to the situation which has led to accusations of complicity. The counter-narrative is that the art being produced is a critique to gentrification and needs to be heard, despite its 'dubious' funding sources. But whether one defines oneself as an 'artwasher' or not, this debate only serves to aid in the *stabilization* of the site for appropriation.

Social housing is being destroyed by a national government intent on applying the traditional Conservative values of a home-owning democracy at all costs (which includes the extension of Thatcher's Right to Buy scheme in 2012). With the persistent popularity of the creative city narrative (exemplified by the London Borough of Culture competition), local councils (in conjunction with the financial backing of property developers and the social responsibility of housing associations) are mobilizing artwashing to acquire social housing, and spread their ideology of land as private, profit-generation machine.

Creative Resistance

So if artists themselves are made complicit with gentrification via artwashing, how can they begin to rearticulate their socially engaged and critical ethics of resistance?

Artwashing has created a fog that obscures artists from clearly seeing how their artistic practices will impact places and their communities. To be artistic and creative in a way that is directly critical of gentrification is increasingly futile because of the sheer adaptability and flexibility of creative capital, and its appropriative capacity. But futility only lingers in the absence of collective action. Yes, the work of individual artists or groups can be co-opted as a vehicle for gentrifying capital, but if connected as part of a broader suite of resistive activities, it can be used to foster alternative, other, perhaps even anti-capitalist spaces.

It is difficult for sure, and the impact may not be felt or seen locally or at that time. But capitalism's growth is dependent upon the continued *dis*aggregation of resistance, creative or otherwise. This process needs to be reversed. Only then can artists begin to regain their ethical and political content as destabilizers.

Resisting the creative city then requires moments of playful and antagonistic rupture, surrounded by a scaffolding of more pragmatic, dare I say, 'official' avenues of resistance. The former act as markers of the problem and they flag the injustices of a capitalist gentrifying system. Take for example Space Hijackers, a group of 'anarchitects' who performed a number of interventionist and subversive activities in London and beyond. They disbanded in 2014 having conducted nearly 100 performances that ranged from their first action, turning a Circle Line Tube train into a disco in 1999, to writing revolutionary text on toilet roll in Canary Wharf bars.[52] Most if not all of their projects were creative reappropriations of the urban environment to highlight a particular politics.

From general critiques of neoliberalism and gentrification to specific causes such as highlighting the privatization of the NHS, Space Hijackers typify the kind of 'creative direct action' that opens up spaces of resistance. One of their more inspired performances was on 16 November 2013, where they undertook what they called a 'Foxtons Hunt'.[53]

Foxtons are a UK-based estate agent, which implement aggressive tactics to market and sell private property. With a particularly high commissioning rate for the sector, Foxtons have become the go-to bogeymen of London's housing crisis.[54] Space Hijackers devised a game in which someone posing as a house buyer would go into a Foxtons and ask to see an expensive property. Once they were being taken to that property in the branded Foxtons car, the rest of the Space Hijackers, dressed in traditional fox hunting attire, would chase after the car on bikes, sounding a hunting horn. They would chase down the car while the fake house-hunter put on a fox's costume. The unsuspecting Foxtons agent would be caught in the middle of the prank.[55]

The Foxtons Hunt was a particularly striking example of urban interventionist activity, not least because of its comedic value. But that fact that it targeted Foxtons and appropriated the traditional practices of the landed gentry makes it a particularly playful and creative critique of *gentri*fication. But in the broader narrative of resistance to the unjust gentrification of London as a creative city, the Foxtons Hunt clearly failed to achieve lasting change.

But that was not the goal. Space Hijackers' manifesto argues that the goal is to change the 'language' of capitalist architecture. They argue:

> We work to confuse as opposed to replace the existing language of architecture. It is not a case of one belief replacing another, but rather a process of corruption takes place. We are not attempting to produce some kind of revolutionary other, which is almost destined to fail.[56]

This 'confusion' (or, in the language I have been using throughout this book, 'destabilization'), then, is a weapon of activism. One that can be used to fuel resistance to produce alternative experiences and subjects beyond capitalism and the creative city it builds. Their refusal to produce a 'revolutionary other' does not detract from the Space Hijackers' agency in aiding to do so.

The Foxtons Hunt didn't result in a moment of 'enlightenment' for the estate agent and a complete reversal of their gentrifying ways. What it did was to use attention-grabbing acts of performative comedy to alert the community to the deeper injustices that Foxtons perpetuate. Without a recognition of the problem in the first instance, how can anyone be expected to begin to act? These small-scale interventionist and creative direct actions 'red flag' the injustices of gentrification; they highlight the problem and mobilize the forces that *can* do something about it. These acts are crucial because they bring media attention. But they are not always so playful. Some are far angrier.

One such example is in Boyle Heights, Los Angeles, a predominately Latino community close to LA's Arts District and therefore a prime location for creative class colonisation. As in Wynwood, Miami, many art galleries (along with the accompanying upmarket coffee shops and luxury-living gated communities) have attempted to open there. What makes this neighbourhood particularly noteworthy is that a small band of militant activists have aggressively protested against any establishment that they deem part of the gentrifying force, and they are particularly attuned to the negative impact of artwashing.

The Boyle Heights Alliance Against Artwashing and Displacement (BHAAAD) have picketed gallery meetings, faced accusations of online and personal harassment, and even thrown faeces at gallery windows.[57] In February 2017, the art gallery PSSST was forced to close after only one year because of constant 'attacks' by protestors and anti-gentrification activists. BHAAAD claimed a significant victory.[58] The group have garnered international attention for their shock tactics: there are reports of them shouting down local theatre performances from external companies, and they even chased urban planning students on walking tours out of the local park.[59] But within these rather extreme activist practices their demands are simple:

new developments are welcome only if they benefit the community as a whole. Their statement about the PSSST closure reads:

> What the community needs instead of galleries [is] authentic affordable housing for low-income people, emergency housing for homeless people and people displaced by gentrification, a laundromat, a needle exchange or harm reduction center, an affordable grocery store, etc. Why was there funding ... to run a gallery to attract new people to Boyle Heights, but not for services for the existing community? Because the forces that backed PSSST never had any interest in Boyle Heights, except as a real estate investment opportunity. This is the tragedy of artwashing: it channels philanthropy into destroying neighborhoods.[60]

Their demands echo those of gentrifying neighbourhoods in the US and across the world (for example, the Balfron Social Club demanded 50 per cent social housing remain after 'redevelopment'). Art galleries can have social utility, of course, when established ethically. But if they are put in place by developers as a tactic to lure in creative class professionals and ultimately displace the social groups who need affordable housing, Laundromats and needle exchanges, they become an invasive force. Protest and activism against these galleries and the gentrifying creative city capital they represent is therefore critical in resisting their socially destructive tendencies. In BHAAAD's case, this is extreme and in some cases indiscriminate, but desperate times call for desperate measures.

BHAAAD's resistance to artwashing, and the creative city process more broadly, can be considered one tactic in a broader set of activism practices. Along with the planning, legal and 'official' political resistance that we see happening in Cressingham Gardens (and plenty of other similar neighbourhoods in London and around the world), these instances of extreme activism are flashes of rage that act as lightning rods for media attention. BHAAAD's actions, while crass and indiscriminate in their targeting of anyone they see as complicit in the gentrifying process, have attracted global media attention.

The same could be said of the attack on the Cereal Killer Café in Shoreditch in September 2015. The Class War activist group organized a protest march through Shoreditch, and by the end, the hipster-run café that sells bowls of cereal for £5 had been seriously vandalized. Global media were quick to condemn Class War as mindless thugs, misguided in their ire toward a small business (even though it was the poster-child of hipsterish, funky, cool and creative Shoreditch-style developments). The group attracted (the obvious) attacks from conservative commentators, but they also suffered critique from other anti-gentrification protestors. Aghast at their shock tactics, some groups who were working in big 'P' political avenues of opposition accused these groups of damaging the credibility of their activist agenda.

However the attention-grabbing practices of BHAAAD, Class War and others viscerally highlight the even more damaging practices of gentrification. They may be vilified and lose sympathy from both 'sides' of the political spectrum, but they bring the injustices of creative city gentrification crashing into the mainstream narrative. They act as foot soldiers of *anti*-gentrification, sacrificing their own credibility and social capital in order to highlight the broader issues. The writer Rob Nixon, when discussing the 'slow violence' of environmental damage and its deleterious impacts on the poor, asks:

> How can we turn the long emergencies of slow violence into stories dramatic enough to rouse public sentiment and warrant political intervention, these emergencies whose repercussions have given rise to some of the most critical challenges of our time?[61]

Despite the dizzying rapidity of gentrification in the world's global cities, it is a similar process of 'slow violence', and is orchestrated by urban management networks to be just so. Artwashing, has (thus far) avoided catastrophic events that demand a socialized, even global response.[62] The slow grind of gentrification upon the urban poor goes on for months, if not years. Specific instances of acute levels of social cleansing may flit in and out of the public consciousness, but rarely do they linger long enough to manifest as direct political intervention. The actions of BHAAAD, Class War and the other 'reactionary' groups rupture that social slumber, drawing opprobrium from some, but highlighting the plight of those marginal subjects being constantly violated by capitalist power structures.

These 'ruptures', either from creative, playful and

subversive interventions (à la Space Hijackers) or street protest are effective, but so too are the more pragmatic and official procedures. The *longue durée* of building alternative spaces outside creative capitalist dogma requires a dismantling, destabilizing and then reconfiguring of those existing spaces. Resistance campaigns are fuelled by the emotional resources gathered from celebratory or reactionary instances of rupture which can be used to tackle the injustices of capitalism head on.

The case of London's skate spot at the South Bank speaks to the 'successful' mobilization of creative resistance. In 2013 one of the UK's most iconic creative and cultural institutions, the South Bank Centre, announced plans to convert a space under the Haywood Gallery, the so-called 'undercroft', into retail outlets. The space has been (and still is) used by skateboarders since the 1970s. It is one of the most well-known and revered skate spots in the world, and understandably the reaction by the skating community to protect it was swift. The Long Live Southbank campaign to save the undercroft achieved its goal of stopping the demolition of the skate spot through a combination of official political campaigning (such as the largest ever planning objection in UK history), clandestine activity (for example, undercover filming of private meetings) *and* creative, artistic practices.[63]

Skateboarding itself is a highly creative act, in that it reappropriates the built environment as an arena of adventure and exploration.[64] Like those who conduct parkour, urban exploration and other urban subversions, they 'see' the city differently; they see a bench as not something to sit on, but as something to grind or kick flip over. So it was inevitable that a creative community such as skateboarders employed artistic practices to aid in the goal of stopping the destruction of their beloved skate spot. Films, art works, in situ performances, music events, poetry, graphic design, fashion: there was a stream of creative content produced by and for the group.

These creative acts sat alongside continual conversations with the South Bank Centre and the local council. When those conversations broke down (which they frequently did), they resorted to more extreme tactics of clandestine filming and gate-crashing closed meetings. The creative products produced told of the anguish and mental exhaustion of the campaigners. The creative content was more than a representation to the wider public of their plight; it was an emotional outlet, a means by which the protestors could vent.

In 2015 the South Bank Centre cancelled their plans. It was an important event in London's cultural politics and sent shock waves through the city's creative industrial sector. It was significant because it showed how subcultural communities can mobilize themselves in a (largely) leaderless collective to take on and defeat gentrification plans by cultural institutions. It was also a crucial reminder that alternative and subcultural spaces *can* exist alongside commercial entities without being constantly threatened by the gentrifying powers of the creative city. It is opening up spaces and allowing the communities and atmospheres they engender to flourish. Indeed, at the time of writing, Long Live Southbank are working to raise the funds to restore the undercroft to its original specifications, having struck a deal with the South Bank Centre. So not only has the space been saved, it is expanding.

Of course skateboarding, and indeed the Long Live Southbank campaign itself, is not immune to appropriation and commodification. Like any other subculture, the lure of fame, fortune and its own mechanisms of injustice still persist (skateboarding still suffers from accusations of the marginalization of women, diffabled people and people of colour). During the campaign, many of these structural injustices were exposed by the gentrifying force and used against them.

For example, Jude Kelly, the artistic director of the South Bank, accused skateboarding of being a middle-class white activity.[65] Although largely inaccurate, it did force introspection from the skaters, and a renewed vigour to address issues within the community. Skateboarding is now a little less homophobic, with openly gay professional skaters, and has more recognition of diffabled and female subjects. While perhaps not directly responsible for this change, the Long Live Southbank campaign did open up conflicting and agonistic spaces and experiences, and undoubtedly this galvanized the UK skating community to be more critically introspective. It then used that new knowledge and self-examination to push back against the dominant creative city narrative.

When discussing the role of artistic and creative practice

and the Occupy movement, the artist Yates McKee has argued that 'collective resistance and collective invention are inseparable'.[66] Art that is utilized within the context of a broader resistance movement not only critiques, it visualizes horizons of possibility. So it was with the Long Live Southbank campaign. The creativity inherent in the campaign allowed them to envision the future of the site as one of subversive creativity in the heartland of London's creative industry landscape.

The countercultural revolution of the 1960s had art and creativity as the fulcrum of their protest practices. But as this book has argued thus far, since then, capitalism has perfected the art of co-option. It was, as political theorist Thomas Frank argued, encapsulated by 'the summary of co-optation theory: "if you can't beat 'em, absorb 'em".'[67] In the half century since, artistic critique has struggled to maintain a consistent voice against divisive and highly adaptive capitalist expansion mechanisms and the injustices they cause. Creative practices that seek to engage communities and social issues are reappropriated for gentrification schemes (now armed with artwashing techniques). Artists are caught in the middle, struggling to balance the need to earn a living and the social ethics of their practice.

The creative city has fine-tuned the 'art' of co-option so efficiently that, to be heard above the noise, resistance needs to have more radical moments. It is no surprise that artists are leading the charge. They are the ones capable of articulated resistance, but also most at risk from falling foul of capitalism's co-option. To give those alternative ethical voices space to be heard, to be acted upon and to help build better worlds, they need to be freed from the noise of a hyped-up, spectacularized and super-mediated system. True creativity is to seek out the tiny voices offering viable alternatives to the injustices of capitalism and, with all the resources available, *collectively* fight against those that seek to appropriate them.

Capitalism's most effective tactic of disarming critique is distinctly neoliberal: it divides the social fabric into individuals, and then pits them against each other. It divides and conquers. By forcing us to look inward just to survive, it blocks the social connections that can help us thrive. To act upon the creative voices that speak of a more just city beyond capitalism, collaborative resistance is vital.

Conclusion
Impossible Creativity

The Queen remarked … 'I'm just one hundred and one, five months and a day.'

'I can't believe that!' said Alice.

'Can't you?' the Queen said in a pitying tone. 'Try again: draw a long breath, and shut your eyes.'

Alice laughed. 'There's no use trying,' she said: 'one can't believe impossible things.'

'I daresay you haven't had much practice,' said the Queen. 'When I was your age, I always did it for half-an-hour a day. Why, sometimes I've believed as many as six impossible things before breakfast.'

Alice through the Looking Glass, Lewis Carroll

If creativity is about the power to create something from nothing, then believing in impossible things is its most critical component. We need to believe that impossible worlds can be reached, if these impossibilities can ever be realized and become lived experiences. But capitalism's rendition of creativity stops this happening. It sells us a different vision of creativity as the *only* possibility. One that is individualized, profitable and autonomous. Such a vision of creativity tempts us, sometimes forces us, to forgo believing in impossible things and instead focus on replicating more of the same: the same inequalities, precariousness, privatization and global injustice that capitalism has thrust upon the world for centuries.

So like the White Queen when confronted with Alice's obduracy, we need practice believing impossible things. Only then can we truly say that we are being creative. So let's practice with one of the most 'impossible' tasks ever undertaken.

On 25 May 1961, the US president, John F. Kennedy, stood in front of Congress and urged them to do the impossible. The USSR had already sent the first dog and man into space, and the US was getting beaten badly in the space race. He said these now famous words:

> I believe that this nation should commit itself to achieving the goal, before this decade is out, of landing a man on the Moon and returning him safely to the Earth.

On 21 July 1969, 163 days before the end of that decade, Neil Armstrong stepped out onto the Moon and was safely back on Earth three days later.

Not only had JFK's most ambitious promises been fulfilled, but he did so by corralling a nation's imagination and excitement and, perhaps more importantly, their tax dollars. The desire to go to the Moon was, clearly, fuelled by the ideological warfare between the US and USSR that nearly threated to obliterate them both during the Cuban Missile Crisis in 1962. JFK took advantage of this heightened period of nationalistic pride to eke out more revenue from a traditionally conservative country to pay for a publicly-funded space exploration programme.[1]

And the US triumphed. It succeeded not *only* in envisioning one of the loftiest, most impossible goals ever by a national government, not *only* in having the temerity to proclaim this out loud to the general public, not *only* in raising the money via public funds; but it achieved the stated goal in the given time frame. It was a global triumph of the collective creative imagination to propel humanity onward on its journey of civilization. It was the belief in, and achievement of, an impossible dream. But perhaps it was the last.

In what is clearly a deliberate reference to the Moon landings, an Alphabet company, named simply 'X', describe themselves as a 'moonshot factory'. X have a blueprint for multiple moonshot projects. They 'look for the intersection of a big problem, a radical solution, and breakthrough technology'.[2] Their projects include driverless cars, online access for millions of unconnected people via internet-enabled balloons that hover in the stratosphere, delivery drones, contact lenses that enable augmented reality, and a host of machine learning products.

These projects in and of themselves could do wonderful things for communities across the world. They could make roads safer, get millions of people online and offer access to information, move things around more efficiently without the need for costly infrastructure, and allow our eyes to see more than just the immediate things around us. But these ideas are being developed within a trillion-dollar corporation: their implementation will be anything but democratic. What is more, by sheer economic force the X lab will eclipse all other public projects in universities and government research labs that are attempting to do similar things, but on much smaller budgets.

X stems from the financial might of Alphabet; they have the room to experiment, and to fail. They can attempt extremely risky and inventive ideas 'whether it leads to the simplicity of a fine invention or the mess of failure'.[3] But the experimentation is yoked to a financialized motive: indeed, X rewards team members who shut down projects that are likely to fail. For all the 'big' thinking and idealism about world-changing inventions and the lip service to the importance of failure, what ultimately counts is the bottom line.

Juxtaposing the Apollo 11 mission and the 'moonshot' projects of X starkly shows how some of the most ambitious ideas that humanity has imagined have been commandeered by capital. We are nearly half a century on from when Neil Armstrong proclaimed that mankind had made a giant leap. Now, any giant leaps we make are dictated by private capital. Creativity has been privatized.

What is more, it's after our collective imagination. Capitalism attempts to stop us from believing in the impossible, or at the very least, reconfigures our imagination so that any realized impossibilities must be profited from first. The very opportunity of an alternative form of creativity and societal organisation beyond capitalism has been all-but foreclosed. This book has shown that our ability to imagine even one impossible alternative, let alone six before breakfast, is being swept away, stolen by capitalism.

But as much as capitalism tries, there will always be a White Queen out there; many in fact. There are always people pushing against capitalism's co-option and privatization of creativity. They are constantly looking to destabilize the ground on which capital thrives. They are creating new ways of working, radically different experiences of the world and entirely new political systems, reaffirming a more ethical and human digital creativity, and building radically creative cities.

Can we take the prompt from these believers? Can we take our lead from the White Queen that there have to be *at least* six impossibilities that we can glean from all this?

Within the realm of work, many traditional organizations of labour protection that rally against the co-optive power of the corporation (such as trade unions) are reactive. They will often only look to restore working conditions of the exploited back to 'normal'. What's required are new ways of organizing that reject this 'normality' in the first place. The co-operative working arrangements that unionize 'autogestively' (outside the traditional trade union model) can push back against the mode of capitalism that sees some workers as disposable and meaningless. They make difficult the smooth functioning of capitalism's exploitation of marginalized and precarious workers. In some cases (as those in Argentina and the *recuperadas*) they even fire their bosses. By treating all workers equally, the exploitative model of capitalism is agitated, problematized and disrupted.

Can these radical democratic processes be scaled up? Defending the traditional labour models against attack is important, but this will only work if viable, more radical alternatives are offered.

Capitalism forces us all to be agile, competitive, individual, flexible and, ultimately, creative. As a result, the world of work has become more precarious, piecemeal and unstable, but at the same time all-consuming. The mindset of 'creative work' has invaded the home, our leisure time and the most intimate reaches of our personal lives. It leaches the resources that would otherwise be directed toward building relationships, resting or playing, and redirects them toward more profitable ends. To defend against this requires more than simply reaffirming what already exists. There needs to be an attempt to shift working patterns toward more co-operative, horizontalized and less marketized forms that we see in pockets of the world around us.

Work is fundamental to our innate humanity: we all have the desire to produce and create, be that things that sustain us, entertain us or bring us closer together. But as Marx and many others since have stressed, capitalism co-opts the value-added for its own. The societal worth of these products is not realized until it has passed through the mechanisms of the market. This ultimately sees that value flow centrally to the elite few.

We can see what a radical version of creative work looks like: we need to replicate it, adapt it, and scale it up to resist capitalism's erosion of the social and communal value of work.

Communal labour models such as those in the NHS in the UK exemplify (albeit under increasing pressure) how socialized labour produces a common good that the whole of society benefits from, regardless of status or wealth. More radical forms of worker co-operatives take this a step further by showing that the fruits of unwaged labour can be mutually exchanged without passing through a system of exploitative markets. These co-ops exist in industry, education and even the retail sector.

This is revolutionary creative work. It exposes the injustices of a capitalist labour system, and points toward, even realizes, a more collaborative horizon, free from the restraints of exploitative waged labour. Those who create these structures are imagining working conditions that would traditionally be thought of as impossible to implement. Within the cracks of a capitalist system are green shoots of revolutionary change. By shunning the individualism that creative work champions, self-managing collectives realize a common labour model, one in which all workers are treated as equals. No matter if they are a cleaner or a 'creative'.

Worker action groups or co-operatives that use 'time banks' are examples of how people create value free from profiteering and marketization. When we work to create that which is commonly consumed, free from monetized exchange and exploitation, this is when we are being radically creative. We are imagining, and making concrete, a system of work that we are constantly told is not viable or possible. We are reifying an impossibility. So, White Queen of Wonderland, that's one.

In addition, there needs to be a redefinition of what it means to be a creative person. This is why we should turn to those who have been forced to the margins of society – in particular disabled, or diffabled, people – and place them at the forefront of progress. The worldly experience of the 'majority' of people is that which capitalism is completely familiar with. After all, advertisers know how to sell things to the 'normal' body. Creative technology producers are familiar with what kind of new apps and video games will appeal to the everyday, typical consumer. But when people experience the world in different ways to that of the majority, or if they have different mental and sensorial capacities to everyone else, then suddenly 'normal' capitalist procedures become unstable.

Diffabled people (physically and/or mentally) experience the world in ways beyond capitalism's comprehension. Deafness, synaesthesia, Tourette's syndrome – they are all conditions that allow people to experience a world others simply cannot access. There is oppression of course; these people are systematically *dis*abled by the workplace, the city, the government, their everyday encounters and personal relationships. But such oppression can come simply from the way the language is constructed. 'Hearing loss' for example; could that be changed to 'Deaf gain'?

How would a different approach – one that viewed these diffabilities as something to be learned from rather than something to cure – lead to spaces and systems of equality? What if we adapted our institutions, cities and workplaces, and tailored them specifically for diffabled people? What would they look like? How would they transform the workplace, the urban realm, the benefits system and virtual spaces?

To answer these questions requires an engagement with the experiences of diffabled people, and crucially to do it *empathetically*; then it can be utilized to destabilize capitalism's growth protocols. Put another way, these experiences can make the stable majority identity distinctly *un*stable.

Creativity doesn't happen in a vacuum. Steve Jobs, Mark Zuckerberg, Charles Darrow and the other 'originals' are eulogized as creative only in so far as they have fed off the creative work of others; context matters. There are particular identity politics at play which, more often than not, privilege white, male, middle-class and able-bodied Westerners. They are able to be creative because they are not using their creativity simply to fight everyday injustices. There is a social network around them to feed, clothe and entertain them; they have not had to use every ounce of their creative energies to fight against institutionalized and everyday sexism, racism and ableism.

Furthermore, neoliberal ideology demands that we individualize. We are told to rely on the self as the sole proprietor of change in the world. Focusing on your interests at the expense of others is the only way to get ahead. Releasing the creative person inside every one of us is how we will all progress as a civilization. But this blinds us to the social worlds that contribute to the imposition of privilege. Neoliberalism hides (and attempts to destroy) the ties that bind us together.

Within this ideological narrative, creativity has become a straightjacket, a character trait that fuels the further imposition of that very same narrative. Sure, everyone is creative, but only those who have 'made it' (those with the privilege) have the luxury of profiting from that creativity. But what they are creating is simply more ways to maintain that division.

So resisting this division, and empathizing with each other and diffabled people, negates this negative form of creativity and proves that a new way is possible. Sharing experiences and stories, we can journey into unknown worlds where, as the chapter demonstrated via some incredible experiences, impossibility simply doesn't exist. That's two, Your Majesty.

And what if we demanded more for our politics? What if we could recalibrate creativity to mean radically altering the way politicians behave? What if being politically creative meant abolishing the current systems and coming up with entirely new forms of government?

Sortition, local currencies, direct action: these are all actually-existing alternative political modes of practice. They have radical forms of democracy in-built. They attempt to foster political engagement. They enact autogestion. They give everyone the opportunity and agency to speak and act. They remove the politics of disavowal and despair. They shorten the 'distance' between a specific desire for change, and realizing it. No wonder they are gaining traction all over the world.

Political regimes across the West are rapidly polarizing. The rise of far-right groups (and indeed, presidents) and their socialist-leaning oppositions has stretched the 'mainstream' political spectrum far wider than it has been for a long time (at least since World War II). This has led to anger and disenchantment; people have taken to the streets in mass protests, marches, riots and artistic practices. The contemporary milieu of protest and activism, while based in a world of political oppression, highlights a real desire for change.

Yet the hyper-mediated creative behaviour of our elected officials masks these 'real' desires and political issues, or repackages them as branding motifs. By aping reality TV, the political realm has been largely disconnected from the public. Too often now we hear of politicians (all over the world) not representing the person on the street. The 'creativity' inherent in politics is more about holding on to power, rather than thinking of new ways of tackling common injustices.

This brand of politics has created governments that have systematically failed to stop – and in some cases, catalysed – inequality, global poverty, environmental degradation and the threat of global nuclear annihilation. As such, people are taking it upon themselves to manage and create new political institutions. If the Arab Spring and the Occupy movement have taught us anything, it's that post-2008, political structures are fragile. The financial crisis may have tightened the iron grip of neoliberalism on everyday life, but it has also brought about a renewed grass roots political awakening.[4]

So within the complex web of governmental politics, clashes of ideologies and economic instability (and the everyday violence perpetuated via austerity), examples of revolutionary political possibility can be seen and experienced. As capitalism's exploitation of, and violence against, the marginalized increases, the seeds of a creative political revolutionary are being sown. What were once seen as political impossibilities (say for example, a socialist in Number 10 or in the White House) are suddenly real possibilities. That's three now isn't it, ma'am?

On top of this political change, we must tackle capitalism's rhetoric of creative technology. The innovations being produced (not least in the X labs) are being created with democratic utility often an afterthought. What if we reversed that trend? What if we started with the premise of democratic governability? What if we asked one simple question before any new app, machine-learning algorithm, or smart city infrastructure were created: how can this be used and managed democratically?

Furthermore, rather than continuing to build complex, autonomous systems that draw humans ever deeper into relationship with code, why not create systems with an 'exit strategy' in place? In other words, we need to make sure that these technological augmentations to our lives are easily removed. We need to make sure we can detach ourselves from them as easily as we can plug ourselves in.

We are now at a point when we have to talk about artificially creative machines for the first time. Classical art can be replicated, human creativity can be learnt very quickly and efficiently, and with the advent of 3D printing, machines have begun to obtain the means of production. Creative technology is progressing extremely quickly. It has the potential to radically change how we work. Automation *can* free up our (increasingly online) work time so we can enjoy our (evermore precious) social time.

That use of technology though will be realized only if progress in what it can do is matched with progress in ethics. Can a machine understand how to undo its own creation? Can we have a machine that understands the damage it does? As Zayep Tufekci said (and is worth repeating) 'we cannot outsource our moral responsibility to machines'.[5]

Human consciousness is being humbled by code, and we need to rebalance this equation before what it means to be human becomes just another piece of software. This may sound alarmist and dystopian but, as we saw, streams of computer code emanating from the tech giants of Silicon Valley in California infiltrate our daily lives via smart personal devices, the surfaces of the city and the things in our homes, workplaces and public institutions. Everything from health services and the police, through to how we find love and how we sleep are controlled by ever-more sophisticated machine learning algorithms. These software-based processes are designed to learn as they go. Computer code can create advertising copy, paint Rembrandts and 3D print complex items. It has ability to adapt to new input, behaviour that is largely hidden from view and, more importantly, from the people that coded them in the first place.

Hence, we are living in an 'algocracy'. Human decision-making is being augmented and, in some cases, supplanted by machine algorithms. Yet, so far, they have not been able to shake off the very human trait of prejudice. We have seen computer algorithms used by the police that mirror institutional racist tendencies, and social media feeds that sift out political material in favour of faddish trends to ensure we stay plugged in. What we see on our social media feeds, the songs we listen to, the information we are presented with, the news sites we visit, the people we meet and the emotions we feel are all beginning to be determined by coded algorithms. While they can bring new things into our consumption patterns ('you listen to X, have you heard Y?'), such creativity serves only to keep us consuming. It is newness to maintain more of the same.

In addition, the sharing economy has enabled us to monetize the things we weren't currently using. Spare rooms, under-used cars and even old wedding dresses can be sold or rented to the highest bidder. We have been promised a more efficient system of resource allocation that has tangible benefits on the reduction of waste but, so far, the sharing economy is being developed so that everything around us that currently isn't making a profit can do so.

The sharing economy is based on the ideology that pervades the corporate culture of Silicon Valley: that autonomy and a complex network of workers, firms, self-employers and ideas realizes more efficient growth. But like every other form of creative technological innovation, it serves only to deepen the precariousness of work except for all but the very privileged few.

Artificial intelligence and creativity have the potential to augment human lives by giving us more free time to engage with agonistic relationships: our family, friends, ourselves. They could produce a world in which an obsession with growth and endless production is a thing of the past. But they need to be created with democracy, the public and the commons in mind. This is now impossible, because of the way capitalism dominates technological production. But it's getting close to breakfast, and we need a fourth impossibility. So this, Your Majesty, is another.

Creativity is so ubiquitous in city development protocols across both the Global North and Global South that it is almost invisible. Every new building, plaza, centre, quarter, zone or district is sprinkled with creativity in the hope that it will attract the creative class and economic 'growth'. Coloured in cool, bohemian and artistic hues, the new city formula of our time depends on a vernacular of creativity.

But what does a creative city look like that isn't any of this? Perhaps more important, how can the creativity embedded in the everyday critique to the hegemony of capital be rescued from the all-co-opting creative city force? Resistance comes in many forms, from militant working class groups, to playful interventions, via institutions that follow more official lines of protest. All these groups and actions have their place in the spectrum of resistance. To be radically creative is to see connections and potential ways of augmenting each path of resistance with the other. To collaborate in opposition is not easy and requires an agonistic mind set of patience, forgiveness, self-restraint and a great deal of emotional energy. Such things are in very short supply in the current suffocating environment of urban capitalism.

This is because the current articulation of the creative city does nothing other than continue gentrification, displacement and violent dispossession. With artwashing, the creative personnel at the leading edge are being used as foot soldiers of this change. Because they have been forced into a precarious life by the unyielding narrative of creative work, artists and creative institutions have no option but to work alongside developers and urban councils. The hope is that the political message gets heard above the noise of the inrushing capital, and it lasts long enough to make a difference. In some cases, these groups are successful (such as the Long Live Southbank campaign), but in others they are less so (as the case of the Balfron Tower exemplified). What is not in doubt, however, is that the creative city discourse has become a unidirectional and homogenising policy tool.

To break free from this mode of thinking is difficult. One might say impossible. But the very fact that there have been victories – that capitalist versions of the city have receded and given way to subversive, public and/or marginal voices and places –proves that a radical creativity is anything but impossible. We're up to five now, nearly there.

Throughout the book, it has been shown that the current doctrine of creativity allows capitalism to disarm its critics by offering them the excitement, stardom and financial rewards that come from succumbing to a market-based system. It calms the agitating forces, chips away at stubbornness, glorifies particular aesthetics of counter-culture, argues that messages can be amplified if only they use market mechanisms. It stabilizes the ground. But these rewards rarely materialize – or if they do, they are short lived or limited to the very few. The rest are left on the margins, exploited and dispossessed. And so the cycle starts once more.

This is not creativity. That is why so many people, groups and ideologies are against creativity. They argue for a more radical interpretation, one that works toward the horizon of impossibility beyond the injustices of capitalism. And they do this by destabilizing the ground and making it infertile to the seeds of capitalism. Of course, this is dangerous, tiring work. The violence inherent in the process of stabilizing the ground has been explained throughout this book. Precariousness, domicide, marginalization, disability, hyper-mediation, austerity, codification, atomization, gentrification, dispossession and many more: creativity as preached by capitalism enacts a 'slow violence' that grinds down any other forms of societal organization, to the chorus of 'there is no alternative'.

But a radical, revolutionary creativity shows that there are alternatives, if we only know where and how to look. Capitalism's greatest lie is getting us to believe that the ground that it seeks to stabilize and profit from is barren and devoid of life. In work, people, politics, technology and the city, creativity is trumpeted as the force that will change the world for the better. Don't believe this lie. Believe that creativity is about searching for, giving space to, and trying to realize the impossible. And that, Your Majesty, is the sixth.

Acknowledgments

There is little point in claiming to have sole authorship of this book, as it has been a collective endeavour between myself and all the people whose work has been an inspiration for the words on these pages. Notably, from the wonderful university department I work in, Mel Nowicki, Pip Thornton, Harriet Hawkins and Innes Keighren. Also of note, Philip Brown, Richard Ocejo, Stephen Pritchard and Dave O'Brien have been a huge help in extracting the ideas out of a thick soup of messy thought and into a coherent argument. And thank you to Paul Richards, Louis Woodhead, Paul Young, Rab Harling, Sofie Narbed, Laura Price, Ben Newman, Jo Cagney, Danny McNally, Ella Harris and the homeless New Yorker whose name I didn't find out – they have been kind enough to share their creativity stories with me. And of course, my utmost appreciation and eternal thanks to Leo Hollis at Verso, who should really be named as a co-author. And for letting me use their Wi-Fi and bringing me free coffee almost daily, a huge thanks to the staff at Costa Coffee in Farnborough Gate.

And thanks to my wife Sarah – her strength, love and dedication have been indispensable through the great times and the not-so-great. In addition, her work for, and dedication to, the NHS was responsible for the direction this book has taken. The NHS is one of the finest creations anywhere in the world, and it is worth fighting for. Finally, my daughters – Jessica and Penny – have shown me entirely new experiences, taken me places I never thought reachable, and we have created new worlds together. Girls, keep on creating!

Notes

Introduction

1 In research for this book, I've found both a Twitter and an Instagram post that have also recounted this anecdote, so clearly the homeless man was a repeat performer.

2 NYC Department for Homeless Services, 'DHS Data Dashboard Charts-FY 2016-Q2', nyc.gov, 2016.

3 The Twitter post that recounts the same story is from April 2017, so I can only assume he is still performing, five years later.

4 I take my lead here from Deleuze and Guattari's understanding of desire. For them, desire is not a want for something lacking (like a new car or a bigger house), but pure productive power. They therefore use the phrase 'desiring-production'. See G. Deleuze and F. Guattari, *Anti-Oedipus*, Continuum, 1984.

5 F. Nietzsche, *The Gay Science*, Vintage, 1974 [1882].

6 R. Sennett, *The Craftsman*, Yale University Press, 2008.

7 M. Haiven, *Crises of Imagination, Crisis of Power: Capitalism, Creativity and the Commons*, Zed Books, 2014.

8 M. Horkheimer and T. Adorno, *Dialectic of Enlightenment*, Stanford University Press, 2002 [1947].

9 Ibid.

10 J. O'Connor, *The Cultural and Creative Industries: A Literature Review*, Arts Council England, 2010.

11 DCMS Creative Industries 'Economic Estimates – January 2016 – Key findings', gov.uk, January 2016.

12 'Biopolitics' is Foucault's term for the way our behaviour (and in some cases, even our psychology) is micromanaged to make us more efficient participants in capitalism (see M. Foucault, *Discipline and Punish*, Pantheon Books, 1977).

13 W. Brown, *Undoing the Demos: Neoliberalism's Stealth Revolution*, MIT Press, 2015, p. 31.

14 This is conceptualized by Joseph Schumpeter as 'creative destruction'.

15 L. Boltanski and E. Chiapello, *The New Spirit of Capitalism*, Verso, 2005.

16 The ad is still available online, youtube.com.

17 O. Solon, 'Kendall Jenner's Pepsi ad criticized for co-opting protest movements for profit', *Guardian*, 5 April 2017.

1. Work: Relentless Creativity

1 In 2004, the UK government made the decision to relocate around half of the BBC's production facilities away from London, in a decision to decentralize creative industry activity from the capital. Salford was chosen over a number of other competing locations. I discuss this process more in my previous book, O. Mould, *Urban Subversion and the Creative City*, Routledge, 2015.

2 W. Whyte, *The Organization Man*, University of Pennsylvania Press, 2013 [1956], p. 35.

3 R. Florida, *Rise of the Creative Class: Revisited*, Basic Books, 2012, p. 45.

4 Ibid. p. 54–5. Florida is keen to point out that structural issues within the creative class are still highly gendered and racialized: white men earn far more than women and people of colour in the same jobs.

5 I outline these critiques in detail in my previous book, but perhaps

the most famous (or at least, most cited) critique comes from J. Peck, 'Struggling with the creative class', *International Journal of Urban and Regional Research*, 2005, 29(4): 740–70.

6 R. Florida, 'Bohemia and Economic Geography', *Journal of Economic Geography*, 2003, 2: 55–71.

7 R. Florida, *The Rise of the Creative Class*, Basic Books, 2002, p. 76.

8 R. Florida, *The New Urban Crisis: How Our Cities Are Increasing Inequality, Deepening Segregation, and Failing the Middle Class – and What We Can Do About It*, Basic Books, 2017, p. xvii.

9 Ibid., p. xviii.

10 This is all shown in a video made by the Institute for Human Activities, an art collective working in the Global South. It can be viewed on vimeo.com.

11 Found on an advert for 'Registered Nurse' at a health and social care charity in Liverpool, 23 August 2017.

12 Found on an advert for a 'Research Assistant' at a leading Russell Group university in London, 23 August 2017.

13 Found on an advert looking for a 'self employed builder' to work on a construction project in St. Albans, 23 August 2017.

14 B. Chapman, 'Subway advertises for "Apprentice Sandwich Artists" to be paid just £3.50 per hour', *Independent*, 20 March 2017.

15 The term 'agile' is increasingly significant in governmental industry policy. Most recently (in the UK at least) in the government's UK Digital Strategy 2017, gov.uk, 1 March 2017.

16 The UK government's latest document on creative industry policy, published in 2016, is entitled 'Create Together: A Creative Industries Council Strategy for Cross Industry Collaboration' (available online). Despite eulogizing collaborative activity, it rarely states how to achieve this beyond classic government-speak platitudes of 'building cross-regional relationships' or 'joined-up practice'.

17 D. Hodgson and L. Briand, 'Controlling the uncontrollable: "Agile" teams and illusions of autonomy in creative work', *Work, Employment and Society*, 2013, 27(2): 308–25.

18 B. Merchant, *The One Device: The Secret History of the iPhone*, Bantam Press, 2017.

19 A story which has been made into a Hollywood film – *The Social Network* (2010).

20 J. Hirsch, 'Elon Musk's growing empire is fueled by $4.9 billion in government subsidies', *Los Angeles Times*, 30 May 2015.

21 The ugly neologism 'playbour' has often been deployed to denote this.

22 D. Spencer, *The Architecture of Neoliberalism: How Contemporary Architecture Became an Instrument of Control and Compliance*, Bloomsbury, 2016, p. 76.

23 R. Florida, *Rise of the Creative Class: Revisited*, p. 105.

24 Although the job security and benefits of university staff are being eroded, as the March 2018 strike by higher education workers highlighted.

25 University and College Union, 'Precarious Work in Higher Education: A Snapshot of Insecure Contracts and Institutional Attitudes', ucu.org, 2016.

26 See G. Kinman, and S. Wray, 'Work-Related Wellbeing in UK Higher Education–2014', University College Union, 2014. This is one of the very few papers that attempt to calculate mental health in academia. There is a general dearth of available information about this, largely blamed on an 'if you can't stand the heat' culture that pervades academia.

27 P. Etchells, 'The human cost of the pressures of postdoctoral research', *Guardian*, 10 August 2017.

28 This ideas is often linked to the idea of a 'delayed' economy, where artists deliberately forgo income, stability and regularity in order to be seen as pioneering artists. See P. Bourdieu, *The Rules of Art*, Stanford University Press, 1998.

29 See A. McRobbie, *Be Creative: Making a Living in the New Culture Industries*, Wiley & Sons, 2016.

30 They're easily available on all good property listing websites.

31 D. Porteous and S. Smith, *Domicide: The Global Destruction of Home*, McGill-Queen's Press, 2001.

32 R. Baxter and K. Brickell, 'For home unmaking', *Home Cultures*, 2014, 11(2): 133–43.

33 The bedroom tax was the phrase coined for the 'Under Occupancy Penalty' policy of the coalition government introduced in 2012. For more details see M. Nowicki, 'Rethinking domicide: Towards an expanded critical geography of home', *Geography Compass*, 2014, 8(11): 785–95.

34 See R. Parreñas, *Servants of Globalization: Women, Migration and Domestic Work*, Stanford University Press, 2001.

35 You can view the footage on bbc.co.uk, 10 March 2017.

36 'Trust cuts 150 jobs at hospitals', BBC News Online, 29 March 2006, and N. Collins, P. Sawer, and J. O'Mahony, 'Mid Staffs report: the key figures in the scandal', *Daily Telegraph*, 5 February 2013.

37 J. Hunt, 'We need to be flexible about the need for flexible working', *British Medical Journal*, 5 July 2017.

38 R. Sennett, *The Craftsman*, Yale University Press, 2008, p. 47.

39 Much of this information I gleaned from informal interviews with GPs, as well as secondary sources such as R. Clarke, *Your Life in My Hands*, Metro Books, 2017.

40 For one striking example of this, see again Rachel Clarke's account of her tenure as a junior doctor.

41 Polls consistently showed the public who thought the doctors were right to strike vastly outnumbering those who thought they were wrong. See W. Dahlgreen, 'Public backing for doctors in government contract dispute', YouGov, yougov.co.uk, 3 February 2016.

42 M. Sitrin, *Everyday Revolutions: Horizontalism and Autonomy in Argentina*, Zed Books, 2012. See also I. Ness and D. Azzellini (eds), *Ours to Master and to Own: Workers' Control from the Commune to the Present*, Haymarket Books, 2012, for a collection of historical and contemporary examples of worker action groups.

43 See I. Ness, *New Forms of Worker Organization*, PM Press, 2016.

44 Coffee Cranks Cooperative, coffeecrankscoop.org.uk.

45 I sourced all these from S. Birch, 'Alternative generation: disenfranchised youth look to co-ops for work', *Guardian*, 31 July 2014. There are no doubt many, many others.

46 D. Matthews, 'Inside a cooperative university', *Times Higher Education*, 29 August 2013.

47 H. Lefebvre, *State, Space, World: Selected Essays*, University of Minnesota Press, 2009, p. 135.

48 Ibid., p. 150.

49 J. K. Gibson-Graham, *Postcapitalist Politics*, Minnesota University Press, 2006, p. 62.

50 Florida, *Rise of the Creative Class: Revisited*, p. 385, my emphasis.

51 Ibid., p. 388.

52 Ibid.

53 K. Marx, *Grundrisse*, Penguin, 1973 [1939], p. 244.

54 D. Harvey, *A Companion to Marx's Capital*, Verso, 2010, p. 46.

2. People: Marginal Creativity

1 The story of Magie is told in far more intricate and fascinating detail in M. Pilon, *The Monopolists: Obsession, Fury, and the Scandal Behind the World's Favorite Board Game*, Bloomsbury, 2015.

2 A. Koestler, *The Act of Creation*, Hutchinson, 1964, p. 35–6.

3 Ibid., p. 177.

4 See T. Barnes, 'A marginal man and his central contributions: The creative spaces of William ("Wild Bill") Bunge and American geography', *Environment and Planning*, 8 May 2017.

5 A. Grant, *Originals: How Non-Conformists Change the World*, Random House, 2016, p. 5.

6 A. Grant, *The Surprising Habit of Original Thinkers*, Ted Talk, February 2016.

7 Yes, they are all men. Deliberately so.

8 Grant, *Originals*, p. 14.

9 For example, see the critical work of A. Ahmed, *Living a Feminist Life*, Duke University Press, 2017.

10 I would absolutely love that not to be the case as it meant that the publishing industry had not thought of partially or fully sighted people as an afterthought, and this may be an audiobook or Braille version.

11 C. Downey, *Design with the Blind in Mind*, Ted Talk, October 2013.

12 See an edited collection by D. Goodley, B. Hughes and L. Davis,

Disability and Social Theory: New Developments and Directions, Palgrave Macmillan, 2012.

13 Michel Foucault's 1963 book, *Birth of the Clinic*, details how centuries of medicalization developed the 'medical gaze', the separation of the body from the person.

14 See L. Mauldin, *Made to Hear: Cochlear Implants and Raising Deaf Children*, University of Minnesota Press, 2013.

15 See for example T. Skelton and G. Valentine, 'It feels like being Deaf is normal': an exploration into the complexities of defining D/deafness and young D/deaf people's identities, *The Canadian Geographer, 2013*, 47(4): 451–66 and G. Harold, 'Reconsidering sound and the city: asserting the right to the Deaf-friendly city', *Environment and Planning D: Society and Space*, 2013, 31(5): 846–62.

16 Quote from Derrick Behm, from 'How architecture changes for the Deaf', youtube.com, 2 March 2016.

17 D. Hebdige, 'Subculture: The Meaning of Style', *Critical Quarterly*, 1995, 37(2): 120–4.

18 C. Codina, O. Pascalis, C. Mody, P. Toomey, J. Rose, L. Gummer and D. Buckley, 'Visual advantage in deaf adults linked to retinal changes', PLOS ONE, 2011, 6(6): 1–8.

19 G. Scott, C. Karns, W. Dow, C. Stevens, and H. Neville, 'Enhanced peripheral visual processing in congenitally deaf humans is supported by multiple brain regions, including primary auditory cortex', *Frontiers in Human Neuroscience*, 2014, 8(177): 1–9.

20 J. Ward, D. Thompson-Lake, R. Ely, and F. Kaminski, 'Synaesthesia, creativity and art: What is the link?', *British Journal of Psychology*, 2008, 99(1): 127–41.

21 J. Denham, 'Jack Coulter: Meet the young artist with synesthesia who "hears" colour', *Independent*, 9 February 2016.

22 N. Harbisson, *I Listen to Color*, Ted Talk, July 2012.

23 Indeed, this is discussed in relation to austerity in the next chapter.

24 That is until this 'flaw' gets ironed out via intensive speech and language therapy.

25 J. Salinas, *Mirror Touch: Notes from a Doctor Who Can Feel Your Pain*, HarperCollins, 2017.

26 Ibid., p. 6.

27 C. Downey, *Design with the Blind in Mind*, October 2013.

3. Politics: Austere Creativity

1 The catchphrase 'You're fired!' from *The Apprentice* almost without any friction at all became 'Lock her up!', 'Drain the swamp!' and 'Make America great again!'

2 For no reality TV series, or indeed major television drama (such as *Game of Thrones*), is complete these days without a related 'discussion' show, usually on a sister channel, hosted by a pseudo-celebrity with a live studio audience. It is no longer enough to mediatize reality any more with one show: the mediation itself has to be the subject of further layers of representation, communication and yet more mediation. Throw in the encouragement of viewers to use social media, and we are presented with an entire circus of signs, misdirection, unreality and media that leaches from the viewer any experiential sense of what the 'reality' was that was being mediated in the first place.

3 For example major environmental disasters exposing the deficiencies of State level provisioning – such as Katrina, Sandy or the 2013–14 winter floods in the UK. Or, indeed, the recent Grenfell Tower fire in June 2017, which exposed the multiple failings of local and national government.

4 *House of Cards*, season 5, episode 12.

5 E. Goffman, *The Presentation of Self in Everyday Life*, Anchor Books, 1956.

6 A. Hill, *Reality TV*, Routledge, 2014.

7 For example, when Trump tweeted about banning transgender people from US military service, it quickly became policy. See A. Ward, 'Trump's ban on transgender troops is now official policy', *Vox*, 25 August, 2017.

8 See M. Fisher, *Capitalist Realism: Is There No Alternative?*, Zero Books, 2009.

9 G. Debord, *The Society of the Spectacle*, Black and Red, 1970 [1967]: Thesis 60.

10 G. Debord, *Comments on the Society of the Spectacle*, Verso, 1990.

11 P. Howard and P. Bradshaw, 'Troops, Trolls and Troublemakers: A Global Inventory of Organized Social Media Manipulation', working paper, Oxford Internet Institute, Oxford University, 2017.

12 See the next chapter for a deeper exploration of this.

13 D. Harvey, *Rebel Cities*, Verso, 2012.

14 I discuss this point in greater depth in O. Mould, 'A Limitless Urban Theory? A Response to Scott and Storper's "The Nature of Cities: The Scope and Limits of Urban Theory"', *International Journal of Urban and Regional Research*, 2016, 40(1): 157–63.

15 Grail Research and de Luxe & Associates, 'Vision Statement: A Map to Healthy – and Ailing – Markets', *Harvard Business Review*, January/February, 2010.

16 W. Davies, *The Limits of Neoliberalism*, Sage, 2014.

17 Ibid.

18 J. Swaine, 'Gordon Brown hails £500 billion bank rescue plan', *Daily Telegraph*, 8 October 2008.

19 Although it is never actually said in these rationales what the prize is for winning this race. Presumably global hegemony of some kind.

20 T. Callan, C. Leventi, H. Levy, M. Matsaganis, A. Paulus and H. Sutherland, 'The distributional effects of austerity measures: A comparison of six EU countries', working paper, No. EM6/11, EUROMOD, Institute for Social and Economic Research, *Guardian*, 2011.

21 S. Campbell, 'Americans live with the austerity you Europeans are so concerned about', theguardian.com, 6 June 2015

22 See M. Blyth, *Austerity: The History of a Dangerous Idea*, Oxford University Press, 2013.

23 Which urban scholars have titled the 'Bilbao Effect' (see O. Mould, *Urban Subversion and the Creative City*, Routledge, 2015).

24 The sponsorship of flagship cultural institutions by large oil companies has been called 'artwashing', see M. Evans, *Artwash: Big Oil and the Arts*, Pluto Press, 2015. I explore this in relation to the city in Chapter 6.

25 It also has a problematic effect on the larger institutions as well but this is also discussed further in Chapter 6.

26 Arts Council (2016), 'Arts Council England: Grant-in-Aid and Lottery distribution annual report and accounts 2015/16', artscouncil. org.uk, 11 July 2016.

27 D. Kean, 'UK library budgets fall by £25m in a year', *Guardian*, 8 December 2016.

28 The Sandal Library in Wakefield became the first 'dementia-friendly' library in the UK when it was 'refitted' in 2015.

29 Forest Hill Library workspace, fhlibrary.co.uk, no date.

30 D. Cameron, 'Big Society Speech' transcript, gov.uk, 19 July 2010.

31 K. McVeigh,'Fit for work assessment was trigger for suicide, coroner says', *Guardian*, 21 September 2015.

32 B. Barr, D. Taylor-Robinson, D. Stuckler, R. Loopstra, A. Reeves, and M. Whitehead, '"First, do no harm": are disability assessments associated with adverse trends in mental health? A longitudinal ecological study', *Journal of Epidemiology and Community Health*, 2016 70(4): 339–45.

33 M. Nowicki, 'A Britain that everyone is proud to call home? The bedroom tax, political rhetoric and home unmaking in UK housing policy', *Social and Cultural Geography*, 2017.

34 R. Rolnik, 'Report of the Special Rapporteur on adequate housing as a component of the right to an adequate standard of living, and on the right to non-discrimination in this context', Office of the High Commissioner for Human Rights, 2013, p. 13.

35 Social Progress Imperative, '2017 Social Progress Index', social progressindex.com, 2017.

36 C. Hermann, 'Neoliberalism in the European Union', *Studies in Political Economy*, 2007, 79(1): 61–90.

37 J. Clarke, A. Huliaras, and D. Sotiropoulos (eds), *Austerity and the Third Sector in Greece: Civil Society at the European Frontline*, Routledge, 2016.

38 K. Bishop, 'What cuts? US austerity "tougher than in Europe"', CNBC News online, 15 November 2013.

39 G. Van Hal, 'The true cost of the economic crisis on psychological well-being: a review', *Psychology Research and Behaviour Management*, 2015, 8: 17–25.

40 D. Stuckler and S. Basu, *The Body Economic: Why Austerity Kills*, Basic Books, 2013.

41 US Department of Justice report 2013, justice.gov, 5 April 2013.

42 R. Florida, *The Rise of the Creative Class*, Basic Books, 2002, p. 315.

43 Ibid.

44 R. Florida, 'The Never-Ending Stadium Boondoggle', CityLab.com, 10 September 2015.

45 In a 'tweet storm' on 8 September 2017, he highlighted how Toronto was in his 'top 3' cities for Amazon to choose. However, he has subsequently stated (during talks for his latest book tour) how the process is rather crass of Amazon, and is symptomatic of the wider problem of what he claims is 'winner-takes-all' urbanism (itself a term curiously similar in concept to the well-established global city thesis). Only to then say that Google's new 'smart city' lab in Toronto will be of huge benefit to the city.

46 Florida, *Rise of the Creative Class*, p. 320.

47 A. Arampatzi, 'The spatiality of counter-austerity politics in Athens, Greece: Emergent "urban solidarity spaces"', *Urban Studies*, 2017, 54(9): 2155–71.

48 A. Cronkright, 'Reinventing student government in Bolivia: Democracy In Practice', Open Democracy, 18 November 2016.

49 Although the new company, Maximus from the US, are not faring much better.

50 UK Uncut, 'About UK Uncut', ukuncut.org.uk, no date.

4. Technology: Algorithmic Creativity

1 Taken from A. Saxenian, 'Beyond boundaries: Open labor markets and learning in Silicon Valley', in M. Arthur and D. Rousseau (eds), *The Boundaryless Career: A New Employment Principle for a New Organizational Era*, Oxford University Press, 1996, p. 23.

2 Ibid.

3 E. Ullman, *Close to the Machine: Technophilia and Its Discontents*, Picador, 1997.

4 A. Saxenian, *The New Argonauts: Regional Advantage in a Global Economy*, Harvard University Press, 2007.

5 F. Foer, 'Facebook's war on free will', *Guardian*, 19 September 2017.

6 As we saw when the UK government used it as a destination for the Creative Industries Task Force in 1998 (as outlined in the Introduction).

7 F. Hayek, *The Road to Serfdom*, Routledge Press, 1944.

8 F. Hayek, 'Competition as Discovery Procedure', *The Quarterly Journal of Austrian Economics*, 2002, 5(3): 9–23.

9 For perhaps the most extreme example of this (that I've come across at least), see M. Rothschild, *Bionomics: The Inevitability of Capitalism*, Henry Holt, 1990.

10 And perhaps not too long beyond that, the singularity.

11 A. Greenfield, *Radical Technologies: The Design of Everyday Life*, Verso, 2017.

12 The phrase is widely credited to a UK mathematician, Clive Humby, in 2006.

13 M. Graham, 'Quant HC tries to predict cardiac arrest with an algorithm', *Chicago Tribune*, 30 March 2015.

14 Emerging Technology (2017), 'Machine-Learning Algorithm Predicts Laboratory Earthquakes', *MIT Technology Review*, technologyreview. com, 3 March 2017.

15 You can see the video of this creation on youtube.com, 12 July 2017.

16 Greenfield, *Radical Technologies*.

17 David Cox, quoted in J. O'Gorman, 'Watch: M&C Saatchi launches artificially intelligent outdoor campaign', campaignlive.co.uk, 24 July 2015.

18 Apart from sign language, for now.

19 It must be noted though that various 'loaded' terms (such as jihad, radicalization and various unmentionable racist slurs) are not offered, and indeed have been used to redirect users to sites that supposedly act to resist the ethics of those terms. So, for example, searching for 'suicide' brings up adverts for the Samaritans.

20 A. Halevy, P. Norvig, and F. Pereira, 'The Unreasonable Effectiveness of Data', *IEEE Intelligent Systems*, 2009, 24(2): 8–12.

21 T. Wu, *The Attention Merchants: The Epic Struggle to Get Inside Our Heads*, Atlantic Books, 2017.

22 The work and creative resistance of the geographer Pip Thornton here is important in understanding how algorithms (particularly Google's marketization via AdWords) are emptying language of any socio-cultural and historical weightiness. See P. Thornton, 'The Death of the Reader', *Under the Influence*, 2017 Spring/Summer: 150–55.

23 See J. Danaher, 'The Threat of Algocracy: Reality, Resistance and Accommodation', *Philosophy and Technology*, 2016, 29(3): 245–68.

24 Greenfield, *Radical Technologies*, p. 89.

25 Ibid., p. 104.

26 Reuters, 'Here's how much Uber made in revenue in 2016', *Fortune*, 14 April 2017.

27 G. Topham, 'Black-cab drivers' Uber protest brings London traffic to a standstill', *Guardian*, 10 February 2017.

28 See M. Bakardjieva, *Internet Society: The Internet and Everyday Life*, Sage, 2015, and J. Ash, *The Interface Envelope: Gaming, Technology, Power*, Bloomsbury Publishing, 2015.

29 A. Sundararajan, *The Sharing Economy: The End of Employment and the Rise of Crowd-Based Capitalism*, MIT Press, 2006.

30 See B. Motofska, 'Why any business can and should participate in the sharing economy', benitamatofska.com, 22 June 2017, no page.

31 Ibid.

32 C. Pooley, 'Deliveroo faces fresh legal action over "worker" rights', *Financial Times* online, 27 March 2017.

33 C. Cant, 'I'm a Deliveroo rider. Collective action is the only way we'll get a fair deal', *Guardian*, 31 March 2017.

34 M. Mauss, *The Gift: The Form and Reason for Exchange in Archaic Societies*, Routledge, 2002 [1950].

35 M. Stroud, 'The minority report: Chicago's new police computer predicts crimes, but is it racist?', The Verge, theverge.com, 19 February 2014.

36 Z. Tufekci, *Twitter and Tear Gas: The Power and Fragility of Networked Protest*, Yale University Press, 2017.

37 K. Gee, 'In Unilever's radical hiring experiment, resumes are out,

algorithms are in', foxbusiness.com, 26 June 2017. 'There's an Algorithm to Fight Online Extremism', sciencefriday.com, 27 June 2017.

38 Z. Tufekci, 'Machine intelligence makes human morals more important', Ted Talk, October 2016.

39 C. Mouffe, *Agonistics: Thinking the World Politically*, Verso, 2013. My emphasis.

40 J. Crary, *24/7*, Verso, 2014, p. 89.

5. The City: Concrete Creativity

1 The video and accompanying documentation regarding applications can be found at london.gov.uk, July 2017.

2 M. Feldman, 'The role of neighborhood organizations in the production of gentrifiable urban space: The case of Wynwood, Miami's Puerto Rican barrio', *FIU Electronic Theses and Dissertations*, digitalcommons.fiu.edu, November 2011.

3 Taken from a video about Wynwood on the BBC News site, bbc. co.uk, 22 July 2014 (although what the BBC are doing hosting what is essentially a promotional video is anyone's guess).

4 See my previous book for some details of the history of this process – O. Mould, *Urban Subversion and the Creative City*. Or for a more comprehensive study see S. Merrill, 'Keeping it real? Subcultural graffiti, street art, heritage and authenticity', *International Journal of Heritage Studies*, 2015, 21(4): 369–89.

5 Quote is from Jonathon Yormak, principal of a New York–based real estate firm, from A. Viglucci, 'With new plan, stakeholders lay out vision for "Wynwood 2.0"', *Miami Herald*, 22 July 2015.

6 The Congress for New Urbanism, based in Chicago, is the main institution responsible for eulogizing this form of urban development.

7 Viglucci, 'With new plan, stakeholders lay out vision for "Wynwood 2.0"'.

8 M. Feldman, 'The role of neighborhood organizations in the production of gentrifiable urban space: the case of Wynwood, Miami's Puerto Rican barrio', *FIU Electronic Theses and Dissertations*, digitalcommons. fiu.edu, November 2011.

9 Quote taken from the Wynwood video, BBC News online, 22 July 2014.

10 N. Smith, *The New Urban Frontier: Gentrification and the Revanchist City*, Routledge, 1996.

11 B. Plaza, 'The return on investment of the Guggenheim Museum Bilbao', *International Journal of Urban and Regional Research*, 2006, 30(2): 452–67.

12 H. Steyerl, *Duty Free Art: Art in the Age of Planetary Civil War*, Verso, 2017, p. 75.

13 Available on youtube.com, 21 June 2012.

14 City of Lincoln, 'Comprehensive annual financial report fiscal year ended August 31, 2016', lincoln.ne.gov, 22 February 2016.

15 This is the common trope used when articulating the Nebraskan economy, a vision that many in Lincoln try to rebuff, see A. Wells, 'TEDxLincoln talks about more than just cows and corn' *Daily Nebraskan*, 14 September 2017.

16 T. Kirk, 'Report: Nebraska worst performing economy in country', *Lincoln Journal Star*, 27 July 2017.

17 I detail this scheme in the opening chapters of my previous book, see Mould, *Urban Subversion and the Creative City*. The document itself is available at cityofsyndney.nsw.gov.au, 29 May 2015.

18 J. Jacobs, *The Death and Life of Great American Cities*, Vintage, 1961, p. 188.

19 A. Markusen and A. Gadwa, 'Creative Placemaking', National Endowment for the Arts, 2010, p. 3.

20 Ibid.

21 See O. Mould, 'Tactical urbanism: The new vernacular of the creative city', *Geography Compass*, 2014, 8(8): 529–39.

22 And indeed are fundamental parts of the creative city critique. For a comprehensive overview see D. Leslie and J. Catungal, 'Social justice and the creative city: Class, gender and racial inequalities', *Geography Compass*, 2012, 6(3): 111–22 and H. McLean, 'Digging into the creative city: A feminist critique', *Antipode*, 2014, 46(3): 669–90.

23 M. Shumow and R. Gutsche Jr., *News, Neoliberalism, and Miami's Fragmented Urban Space*, Lexington Books, 2016.

24 M. Fisher, *Capitalist Realism: Is There No Alternative?*, Zero Books, 2009.

25 McLean, 'Digging into the creative city: A feminist critique'.

26 Ibid, p. 686.

27 Ibid.

28 M. Evans, *Artwash: Big Oil and the Arts*, Pluto Press, 2015.

29 C. Wu, *Privatising Culture: Corporate Art Intervention Since the 1980s*, Verso, 2003.

30 *Ibid.*

31 *Channel 4 News*, 'BP protest: "Tate should come clean about dirty oil money"', channel4.com, 20 April 2011.

32 F. Zimring, *The City that Became Safe: New York's Lessons for Urban Crime and Its Control*, Oxford University Press, 2011.

33 M. Greenberg, 'Tenants Under Siege: Inside New York City's Housing Crisis', *New York Review of Books*, 17 August 2017.

34 D. Hill, 'London's homelessness count continues to rise', *Guardian*, 1 December 2016. The number has only increased since.

35 P. Sng, dir, *Dispossession: The Great Social Housing Swindle*, Velvet Joy Productions, 2017.

36 A. Minton, *Big Capital: Who Is London for?*, Penguin Books, 2017.

37 Ibid.

38 S. Pritchard, 'Artwashing: Social Capital and Anti-Gentrification Activism', *Colouring in Culture* blog, 17 June 2017, no page.

39 O. Mould, 'Why culture competitions and "artwashing" drive urban inequality', Open Democracy, 14 September 2017.

40 A process perhaps first written about extensively in T. Wolfe, *The Painted World*, Farrar, Straus & Giroux, 1975, and S. Zukin, 'Loft living as "historic compromise" in the urban core: The New York experience', *International Journal of Urban and Regional Research*, 1982, 6:256–67

41 J. Ellior, 'The Job Centre bar's attempt to do gentrification ironically is an insult', *Guardian*, 9 July 2014.

42 E. Whitford, 'New Crown Heights restaurant proudly advertises cocktail next to "bullet hole-ridden wall"', gothamist.com, 18 July 2017.

43 J. Butler, 'Social Cleansing in Tower Hamlets: Interview with Balfron Tower Evictee', novaramedia.com, 20 August 2013.

44 'Balfron Tower, Poplar: "They all said the flats were lovely"', municipaldreams.com, 21 October 2014.

45 The video was recorded before it was taken down and can be seen at 50percentbalfron.tumblr.com.

46 B. Mortimer, 'How the Balfron Tower tenants were "decanted" and lost their homes', *East End Review*, eastendreview.co.uk, 24 March 2015.

47 Which can be found online here: simonterrill.com.

48 Felix Mortimer, quoted in C. Bedei, 'Overnight Macbeth play at Goldfinger's Balfron Tower', eastlondonlines.co.uk, 20 July 2014. H. Ellis-Petersen, 'Decaying east London tower block to house 12-hour Macbeth production', *Guardian*, 19 July 2014.

49 A project he later released as 'Inversion Reflection', which he presented at the Royal Geographical Society in August 2014, a version of which can be found on vimeo.com, 26 August 2014.

50 See the @BalfronSocial twitter feed and his blog, notably the blog post 'Balfron Tower: The Artwash of an Icon' on 50percentbalfron. tumblr.com.

51 H. Nicklin, 'Artwashing', poplarpeople.co.uk, 9 March 2016.

52 An archive of their projects can be found here: spacehijackers.org.

53 D. Graeber, 'The New Anarchists', *New Left Review*, 13 January-February, 2002.

54 G. Norwood, 'Revealed – the pay and commissions paid by Foxtons', estateagenttoday.co.uk, 18 July 2015.

55 This is described in detail at spacehijackers.org.

56 Space Hijackers 'Second Manifesto of the Space Hijackers', 2011.

57 C. Miranda, '"Out!" Boyle Heights activists say white art elites are ruining the neighborhood ... but it's complicated', *Los Angeles Times*, 14 October 2016.

58 A. Lloyd, 'PSSST Gallery closes in Boyle Heights amid anti-gentrification battle', laist.com, 22 February 2017.

59 N. Delgadillo, 'The neighborhood that went to war against gentrifiers', citylab.com, accessed 1 March 2017, and R. Carroll, '"Hope

everyone pukes on your artisanal treats": Fighting gentrification, LA-style', *Guardian*, 19 April 2017.

60 BHAAAD, Statement from Defend Boyle Heights and BHAAAD on PSSST closing, alianzacontraartwashing.org, no date.

61 R. Nixon, *Slow Violence and the Environmentalism of the Poor*, Harvard University Press, 2011, p. 3.

62 Although the Grenfell Tower fire in the summer of 2017 is beginning to take shape as a critical juncture in the gentrification debate. The investigation (arguably not far-reaching enough) has yet to be completed but will no doubt show the Grenfell tragedy to be a perfect storm of unjust gentrifying, and neoliberal and austerity practices.

63 I have discussed this campaign in detail elsewhere in my previous work, including *Urban Subversion and the Creative City*.

64 I. Borden, *Skateboarding, Space and the City: Architecture and the Body*, Berg, 2001.

65 L. Woodhead, 'Underdeveloped, underused and undernourished – getting inside the mind of an arts institution struggling to keep up with the times', llsb.com, 15 August 2014.

66 Y. McKee, *Strike Art: Contemporary Art and the Post-Occupy Condition*, Verso, 2016, p. 16.

67 T. Frank, *The Conquest of Cool: Business Culture, Counterculture, and the Rise of Hip Consumerism*, University of Chicago, 1998, p. 7.

Conclusion

1 Final estimates put the whole cost of the Apollo missions at $25.4bn.

2 X, 'What We Do', x.company, no date.

3 D. Thomson, 'Google X and the Science of Radical Creativity', *The Atlantic*, November, 2017.

4 A. Badiou, *The Rebirth of History*, Verso, 2010.

5 Z. Tufekci, 'Machine intelligence makes human morals more important', Ted Talk, October 2016.

Index

Index

Index

Index

Index